A LANCASTER EPHEMERA
Printed Relics from a City of Letters

A LANCASTER EPHEMERA
Printed Relics from a City of Letters

SIMON HAWKESWORTH

Fast Foot Press

Lancaster

www.fastfootpress.co.uk

2014

A Lancaster Ephemera: Printed Relics from a City of Letters, by Simon Hawkesworth.

First published in Great Britain in 2014 by Fast Foot Press.

British Library Cataloguing in Publication Data. A catalogue record for this book is available from the British Library.

ISBN: 978-0-9571922-3-2

Printed by Wallace Printers of Bolton, Lancashire, using Conqueror, Trophée and Fedrigoni stocks, and bound by Sanderson of Preston, Lancashire. Set in Arno and Whitney typefaces.

Fast Foot Press is an independent publisher and design studio. Based in Lancaster, it develops publications relating to social history, architecture, the arts and design.

Fast Foot Press

18, Hastings Road, Lancaster, LA1 4TH

w: www.fastfootpress.co.uk — e: info@fastfootpress.co.uk

immon Clayton & Sons

BROCK STREET CYCLE DEPOT,

LANCASTER.

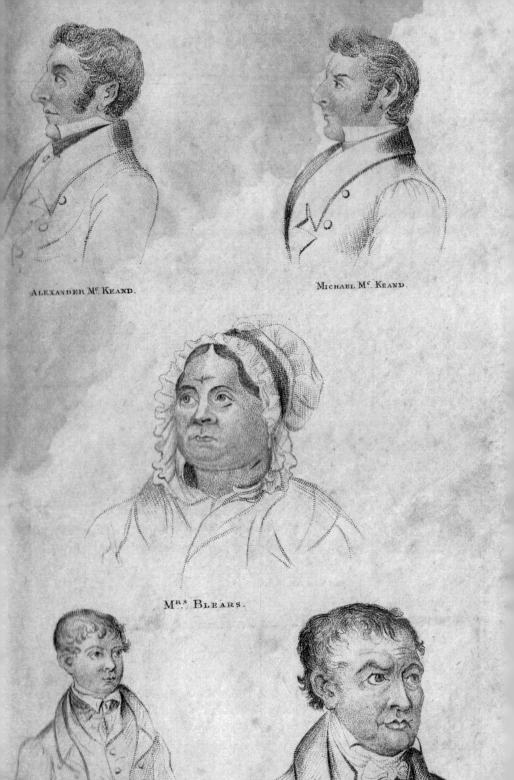

ALEXANDER M^C.KEAND.

MICHAEL M^C.KEAND.

M^{RS} BLEARS.

In memory of Alan Bartram, 1932–2013: writer, book
designer, artist and inspiration.

CONTENTS

PREFACE

This book, and my growing fascination with printed ephemera, began by accident while researching for a previous publication. Hunting through the archives of Lancaster Public Library, I came across collections of broadly-catalogued documents, leaflets, old handbills, public notices and event programmes. Not only were these invaluable sources of information about the buildings and memorials that I was researching, but I began to realise that these papers revealed a wealth of cultural, social and typographic information about Lancaster. Each document is a small window into the past, revealing snatches of the lives of the people and the events of the city from as far back as the seventeenth century. In the process of these discoveries a whole new world of information had opened up to me, and an infectious love of printed ephemera developed. It is a contagion that this book hopes to impart to others.

Simon Hawkesworth
Lancaster
2014

INTRODUCTION

....

Printed ephemera encompasses items as diverse as posters, leaflets, event programmes, packaging, newspapers, receipts and a host of other materials. Indeed, despite the increasing impact of digital technology on our lives, the inspection of any household letterbox will provide an almost daily delivery of paper items that include newspapers, takeaway menus, parish newsletters, double glazing offers and a myriad of advertisements. Designed mainly as temporary solutions to everyday needs, they seldom survive much beyond their immediate use. Most are, by any standards of design and aesthetics, ugly, transient pieces of paper flotsam. Yet these fragile and often poorly printed items can provide us with a sense of history and a glimpse into the social, economic and design preoccupations of a particular time. It's only with the benefit of hindsight that we often appreciate their value, and by then of course, they have usually been disposed of.

The examples of ephemera given in this work were obtained in most part from the archives of Lancaster Public Library—specifically

its excellent Community Heritage Centre. They span a period from the middle of the seventeenth century until the present, although the majority are from the nineteenth century, and include items relating to commerce, politics, public information and the world of entertainment.

These simple pieces of paper provide insights into the many features of the city's rich history and the world beyond. Some represent well-known aspects of Lancaster's past, including those advertising renowned industries such as the flooring manufacturers Storey Brothers or the glassmakers Shrigley and Hunt. Others are more obscure but no less intriguing. These include documents detailing public executions, warnings to itinerant traders, or notices prohibiting the standing of cattle on public highways— all of which seem disconnected from our modern world. A number relate to the justice system (Lancaster was, for over three hundred years, the location of the regional assizer court). These items provide an insight into the often precarious nature of life during the nineteenth century. It's hard not to be moved by the harsh sentences detailed on handbills for offences as trivial as petty theft, when the taking of a handkerchief might mean transportation or even death.

Many items include the names of the local printing firms that created them. In addition to more well-known printers such as Clark and Milner, we also find reference to those of Bell, Brash, Busher, Eaton & Bulfield, Holme & Jackson, Jackson, King, Minshull and Watkinson, and in doing so we learn a little more of the people and businesses that underpinned this important industry.

A few items speak of events beyond Lancaster. There is the handbill of 1819 in which local dignitaries warn of 'seditious and mischievous doctrines' as the news of the Peterloo Massacre, and its implications for the social order, reach Lancaster. Or the pamphlet of 1802, written in defence of Napoleon Bonaparte, that lambasts the editor of a local paper for his criticism of the self-proclaimed First Consul of France. In addition to these polemics there are songs printed on flimsy sheets of paper that speak of ships and ports and trade, revealing the growing links that Lancaster forged with the world around it during the eighteenth and nineteenth centuries.

Local politics are also addressed in handbills concerning elections, broadside ballads that question the morality of the powerful, illustrations mocking political opponents, and a magnificent Chartist poster invoking the rebellious spirit of a dead leader.

As well as the historical events that they relate to, these printed relics are full of intriguing idiosyncrasies, archaic language and the trivia of everyday life. We hear the words and preoccupations of a different age in the use of 'hucksters and higglers', 'forenoon', 'assize', 'parker's special smoking mixture', 'james powders', 'analeptic pills', and 'clinchers', 'seddons' and 'boothroyds' (bicycle tyres). There are also the people themselves.

The wealthy and the destitute, the famous and the infamous, the known and the forgotten: Charles Wilkinson, Obadiah Marland, James Williamson, Elizabeth Dean, J. S. Slinger, Alex and Michael McKean, Elizabeth Blears, Karel Klíč, Richard Parker, T. D. Smith, Bartholomew Baines, Betty Brindle, Alexander Andrade, Richard Fawcett, Fergus O'Connor and many more.

These ephemeral items are also interesting from a typographical perspective in that they provide examples of many of the typefaces commonly used at the time of their production. From the eighteenth and early nineteenth centuries we find Old Faces, Transitional typefaces and the emergence of both the Fat Faces and Ornamented lettering that were used for titling. In the later part of the nineteenth century we see advertisements composed from a menagerie of different typefaces. Here a multitude of varied letterforms were used in the hope of catching the eye and loosening the purse. By the early twentieth century we encounter printed ephemera influenced by the styles of the Arts and Crafts and Art Deco movements. Later items, such

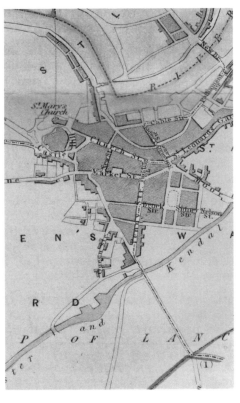

as screenprinted posters advertising Lancaster's extensive music scene, banners used in demonstrations, or the draft manuscripts of local writers show the use of handwritten and illustrated approaches to conveying the written word.

Several of the items presented are not strictly ephemera; being materials that were intended to have some longevity. However, the things that these items originally described have largely ceased to be, including organisations or companies, events lost to local memory, or places changed beyond recognition. The maps that are included, as well as being beautiful objects in themselves, provide some of the most striking indications of the way in which places change, reminding us that the landscape we inhabit is also transient.

The examples presented in this collection are printed relics from the past, existing only because some far-sighted librarian, archivist or collector decided to preserve them for future discovery, discussion and comment. Much of the history of Lancaster is written in these kinds of ephemeral objects—a city made of letters, words, ink and wood pulp. By following the 'paper trail' left by these fragments we can explore the often forgotten histories of the city.

Illustration from a souvenir brochure concerning
the attractions of Lancaster, 1897

EPHEMERA

An important factor in the development of Lancaster was its location as the site of the Assizer Court. Here travelling judges would try cases and pass sentences on defendants from across the region. It not only elevated the status of the town but had an important social, architectural and economic impact, as an infrastructure developed around the judicial process. This document of 1659 confirms the establishment of the assizes through an Act of Parliament.

The printer of this Act, John Field, became the printer to Parliament during the turbulent period of the mid to late 1600s. Along with Henry Hills, Field gained a near monopoly over bible printing during the same period. Field's close association with Oliver Cromwell, rather than his printing expertise, is regarded as the most likely reason for the lucrative positions he obtained.[35] Indeed, the error that can be seen in the title of the document shown here (the double letter S in the word 'Assize' is upside down) is perhaps indicative of the problems associated with Field's craft. His most notorious typographic error was the so-called *Unrighteous Bible* of 1653 in which I Cor. 6:9 reads, 'Know ye not that the unrighteous shall inherit the kingdom of God?', the word *not* having been omitted after the word *shall*.

An Act for Holding an Assize for the County of Lancaster

Printer: John Field, London

1659

An Act for Holding an Assize for the County of Lancaster
Parliamentary Act

AN ACT

For holding an

ASSIZE

For the County of

LANCASTER.

Friday, Auguſt 5. 1659.

ꝛRdered by the Parliament, That this Act be forth-
with Printed and Publiſhed.

TWO
SERMONS

Preached at the

ÄSSIZES

HELD AT

LANCASTER,

ON

Sunday Aug. 27. 1710.

And at Several other Places.

BY

HENRY RICHMOND,
Rector of *Leverpoole,* and Chaplain to
the Right Honourable, ELIZABETH,
Counteſs Dowager of *Derby.*

Publiſh'd at the Requeſt of the Gentry and
Clergy, the *Grand-Jury* being diſcharg'd on
Saturday Night.

LONDON:
Printed for *Jonah Bowyer,* at the *Roſe* in *Lud-
gate-ſtreet,* and Sold by *Joſeph Eaton* Book-
ſeller in *Leverpoole,* 1710.

Two Sermons Preached at the Assizes Held at Lancaster
Assize Sermons

A regular occurrence at the assizes was the preaching of sermons by the clergy and the publication of the event in the form of a pamphlet. It was not only part of the ritual of the proceedings but an opportunity for the clergy to make a connection between the criminal justice system, morality and religious tenets. The sermons were civic events that were closely tied to the religious and political structures of the period.

These sermons are by Henry Richmond, Rector of Liverpool (Leverpoole), for the assizes held at Lancaster on 27th August, 1710. Henry was the son of Sylvester Richmond, a noted physician who was born in Garstang near Lancaster, and who become Mayor of Liverpool in 1672.[38] Henry was not only a member of the clergy but was active in Liverpool politics and a strong supporter of the Earls of Derby; the powerful Liverpool landowners and political figures who held the offices of Chancellor of the Duchy of Lancaster and Lord Lieutenant of Lancashire.[42]

The pamphlet was printed for the publisher Jonah Bowyer at Ludgate Street, an area of London long associated with booksellers and printers.[46] The 'Rose' in the address refers to the signage on the streets at the time, by which the location of a business could be found before the widespread use of street numbers. The pamphlet was sold by the Liverpool bookseller, Joseph Eaton.

Cover of a pamphlet giving the details of two sermons held at the Lancaster Assizes

Printer: Unknown

1710

RICHARD PARKER,

GROCER, BOOKSELLER, STATIONER,

AND

DEALER in SPIRITUOUS LIQUORS,

UNDER A GRATEFUL SENSE OF THE FAVOURS HE HAS RECEIVED

FROM HIS FRIENDS,

BEGS LEAVE TO ACQUAINT THEM

That he is removed from the Corner of the TOWN's HALL,

INTO A

Large and commodious SHOP in New-Street,

Late in the Possession of Mr. EDWARD ATKINSON, Ironmonger;

WHERE HE HOPES TO MEET WITH A

Continuance of the kind SUPPORT of his FRIENDS and the PUBLIC

IN GENERAL.

―――――――――

N. B. *RICHARD PARKER is the Sole* VENDER

IN THIS TOWN, OF

Dr. JAMES's POWDER, and ANALEPTIC PILLS

By Mr. FRANCIS NEWBERY's Certificate.

DEALER ALSO

IN ALL OTHER GENUINE MEDICINES.

LANCASTER, November 12th 1791.   A. BUSHER, Printe

This handbill by one Richard Parker, advertises the
re-establishment of his shop at new premises on
New Street. What is perhaps surprising is the range
of services Mr Parker is providing, being not only a
grocer, but a seller of books, stationery, medicines and
spirituous liquors. It must have been an impressive
(though possibly overwhelming) array of goods that
included 'James's Powders', a successful patent medicine
of the period that was developed by Dr. Robert James
(1703–1776), a physician and friend of Samuel Johnson.

Something of the multifaceted nature of business
occupations at this time is also shown in the work of
the printer, Ambrose Busher (–1796).[11] Busher, located
in the adjoining Market Street, was also an author,
publisher and an active Freemason. As well as the kind
of jobbing printing seen in this handbill, his company
printed and published books of sermons, works on
Freemasonry, political tracts and historical texts.

Handbill advertisement for the
business of Richard Parker

Printer: A. Busher

1791

Richard Parker, Grocer, Bookseller, Stationer and Dealer in Spirituous Liquors
Handbill

Public notice relating to trading in

the town's marketplace

Printer: Unknown

1796

The charter of 1193, which acted to establish the Borough of Lancaster, also granted the right to hold a market in the town. Market traders were later required to pay the Town Council for the privilege of selling their goods.[6] This public notice, printed in 1796 and distributed by the Mayor, is a warning to those 'hucksters and higglers'—itinerant merchants—who might disrupt the normal working of the market. These merchants sought to buy the produce of the market traders in the morning in order to sell them on later at inflated prices. To try and prevent this, it was strictly prohibited to purchase goods from the market before 11 o'clock in the *forenoon* (another wonderfully archaic word); and this notice gave warning that those who did so would be 'prosecuted, with the utmost rigor of the law'.

Huckster or Higglers
Public Notice

...rough of La...

WHEREAS several Hucksters...
have made a Practice of buy...
Justice and other Privileges, ...
...to sell the same again, to the gr...
...and Detriment of the Inhabitants...
...first to have an Opportunity...
...selves therewith, from the Market...

...is therefore hereby giv...

...HUCKSTERS or HIGGLERS, s...
...to buy any of the above-ment...
...ket before the HOUR...
...noon, they will be prosecu...
...of the Law.

Mr. MAYOR

...JANUARY...

For the BENEFIT of

M.ᴿ SIDDONS

THEATRE, LANCASTER.

On MONDAY next, September 1ſt, 1800,

Mr. SIDDONS preſents his beſt Reſpects to the Ladies, Gentlemen,
and the Public at large, and is extremely ſorry, that from indiſpenſible
Concerns, he is obliged to advertiſe his Benefit at ſo early a Period of
the Seaſon; he however flatters himſelf he ſhall be honoured with the
ſame Patronage he has uniformly experienced from the Audience of
Lancaſter.—The Play fixed on for this Evening is

THE CELEBRATED TRAGEDY OF THE

REVENGE:

OR,

The Prince of Africa.

WRITTEN BY DR. YOUNG, AUTHOR OF THE "NIGHT THOUGHTS," &c.

Zanga, (Prince of Africa)   Mr. SIDDONS
(The LAST NIGHT BUT ONE of his performing in Lancaſter this Seaſon)

Carlo,	Mr. SEYMOUR
Alvarez,	Mr. DAWSON
Manuel,	Mr. NICHOLSON
Officer,	Mr. MAYCOCK
Don Alonzo, (the Spaniſh General)	Mr. REMINGTON
Iſabella,	Mrs. REMINGTON
Leonora,	Mrs. DAWSON

BETWEEN THE PLAY AND FARCE,

A Comic Poetical Sketch, written by Mr. SIDDONS, called,

PEEPING TOM'S

Peep into Lancaster,

In which will be deſcribed all the principal Places in LANCASTER
and its ENVIRONS,

To be Spoken in Character,

By Mr. CRISP.

(By Deſire) COLLINS's ODE on

The PASSIONS,

Will be recited by Mr. SIDDONS.

TO CONCLUDE WITH THE ADMIRED MUSICAL FARCE OF THE

BABES in the WOOD:

Or, The Cruel Uncle.

Walter,	Mr. SIDDONS
Apathy,	Mr. DAWSON
Lord Alford,	Mr. SEYMOUR
Oliver,	Mr. MAYCOCK
Sir Rowland,	Mrs. NICHOLSON
Gabriel,	Mr. CRISP
Joſephine,	Mrs. CRISP
Winifred,	Mrs. REMINGTON
Helena,	Mrs. DAWSON
Children,	the Miſs DAWSONS

Tickets to be had of Mr. SIDDONS, at Mr. Steele's, Green Area, and at Mr. JACKSON's,
Printer, Market Place, Lancaſter, where Places for the Boxes may be taken.

For the Benefit of Mr Siddons
Theatre, Lancaster
Handbill

Known originally as simply The Theatre, the Grand
Theatre as it is now called, is reputed to be the third
oldest in Britain. It has been in near continuous use
since 1782, when it was first opened by Joseph Austin
and Charles Edward Whitlock. The famous actor, Sarah
Siddons (1755–1831), Whitlock's sister-in-law, played
Lady MacBeth there in 1795.[4]

This handbill of 1800 advertises a programme
offering: *The Revenge: or The Prince of Africa, Peeping
Tom's Peep into Lancaster, The Passions* and *Babes in the
Wood: Or The Cruel Uncle.* The actor and playwright
Henry Siddons (1774–1815), the eldest child of Sarah,
features prominently on the bill. Henry worked in
theatres across Britain before becoming a theatrical
manager.

By 1830 the theatre was used mainly as a meeting
place for temperance societies, and later, as a music
hall. In 1857, Charles Dickens, while touring with
Wilkie Collins, appeared here. In 1860 it became the
Athenaeum under the ownership of local architect
Edmund Sharpe (1809–1872), and later the
Athenaeum Theatre when control passed to Henry
Wilkinson. The remodelling of the building in 1897
by the renowned theatre architect, Frank Match, was
undone by a severe fire in 1908. After being rebuilt it
became the Grand Theatre. Saved from demolition in
1951 by the organisation Lancaster Footlights,[4] the
Grand continues under their management and care to
host both professional and amateur productions, as well
being a venue for comedy, dance and music.

Handbill advertising events at
The Theatre, Lancaster

Printer: Jackson

1800

General Court Martial of Colonel John Fenton Cawthorne
Details of Proceedings

Cover of a pamphlet detailing the events of the general court martial of Colonel John Fenton Cawthorne, held between November 1795 and January 1796

Printer: Clark

1802

John Fenton Cawthorne (1753–1831) has something of the Dickensian villain about him. Born into a wealthy family, and having trained as a barrister, he was known for his unpleasant disposition and a reactionary disagreement with progressive politics. Cawthorne opposed the abolition of slavery and it is reported that on his country estate, he organised an annual burning of an effigy of the radical writer, Thomas Paine (1737–1809).[15] Cawthorne is also one of the signatories to the public notice of 1819 that was produced in opposition to the growing call for voting liberalisation (p.45).

In 1796, while serving as a Colonel in the Westminster Militia, he was court martialled and found guilty of fraud. The trial adjudged that he be '…cashiered, and declared unworthy of serving His Majesty in any Military Capacity whatever. Also, that by order of the King: '…the House of Commons by their Vote of Expulsion deemed the Subject of these Proceedings, who was then a Member, unworthy of a Seat in that Assembly….' As a result, Cawthorne was expelled from Parliament, losing the seat that he had held for Lincoln since 1783. Yet despite what might be considered an indelible stain on his character, he became the Tory MP for Lancaster in 1806, and again in 1812, 1820 and 1824.[41]

This edition of the proceedings was reproduced in 1802 by the Lancaster printer, Clark, perhaps indicating a continuing local interest in the affairs of this notorious figure.

THE

SENTENCE

OF A

GENERAL

COURT MARTIAL,

HELD AT

THE HORSE GUARDS,

UPON

olonel John Fenton Cawthorne,

OF

The Westminster Regiment of Militia,

On Friday 27th November, 1795.

Cover of a pamphlet produced
in response to the editor of the
Lancaster Gazetteer

Printer: J. Jackson

1802

This remarkable document was written in 1802 and
is addressed to the editor of the *Lancaster Gazetteer*.
The author, who writes under the name of Phocion,
takes issue with the newspaper's treatment of General
(Napoleon) Bonaparte, believing that the *Gazetteer*'s
stance is not only 'so contrary, so diametrically opposite
to the general tenor of that young Hero's conduct', but
endangers a pending treaty of peace and commerce
between France and Britain (probably the Treaty of
Amiens). The newspaper editor, Phocion believed, was
guilty of 'raking up and exaggerating transactions to
the prejudice of a character to which I have no doubt
the faithful page of the historian will do ample justice'.
The pamphlet is a spirited, though uncritical defence
of Bonaparte and the new Republic, citing quotes from
Bonaparte's letters and speeches. Despite the treaty,
peace was short-lived, and hostilities resumed in 1803
when Britain declared war on France.

A Sketch of the Character of General Bonaparte in Letters to the Editor of the Lancaster Gazetteer
Pamphlet

A
SKETCH
OF THE
CHARACTER
OF
EN. BONAPARTE,
IN LETTERS

o the Editor of the LANCASTER GAZETTEER:

WITH

SPECIMENS
OF HIS

Speeches, Proclamations, &c,

AND HIS

LETTER
TO THE

KING,

ON BEING CALLED TO THE IMPORTAN

OF

First Magistrate

OF THE

FRENCH REPU

London,

Printed by J. _____ ___ ____

This patriotic song was written by the Scot, Thomas Campbell (1774–1844) around 1800,[45] at a time when war with Russia seemed likely. The song was widely distributed across the country, and is one of many broadsides printed in the town during the late eighteenth and early nineteenth centuries that testify to Lancaster's strong maritime links and its role as both a port and a shipbuilding town.

During this period, Lancaster developed strong trading links with the West Indies and with ports in mainland Europe, with ships arriving at the quay to off-load goods such as cotton, rum and hardwoods. Prominent firms such as Gillow & Co. traded in high quality furniture, with wood being imported from the Americas and finished products exported across the world. Lancaster also played an important role in the slave trade, and there is evidence of slaves being established as servants in the town.[31] Many ships were built at the town's shipyards, both traders and warships, before Lancaster's maritime industry eventually began to decline.

Ye Mariners of England
Broadside Ballad

YE

Mariners of England.

YE mariners of England,
  Who guard our native seas,
Who for these thousand years have brav'd
  The battle and the breeze—
Your glorious standard launch again,
  And match another foe,
And sweep through the deep,
  While the stormy winds do blow.
While the stormy winds do blow,
  While the stormy winds do blow,
While the battle rages long and loud,
  And the stormy tempests blow.

The spirits of your fathers
  Will start from every wave ;
The deck it was their field of fame,
  The ocean was their grave.
Where Blake, the boast of freedom fought,
  Your manly hearts will glow,
As you sweep through the deep,
  While the stormy winds do blow.
          While the stormy winds, &c.

Britannia needs no bulwarks,
  No towers along the steep :
Her march is o'er the mountain-wave,
  Her home is on the deep ;
With thunder, from her native oak,
  She quells the floods below,
As she sweeps through the deep,
  While the stormy winds do blow.
      :   While the stormy winds, &c.

The meteor-flag of England
  Must yet terrific burn,
Till the stormy night of war depart,
  And the star of peace return ;
Then to our faithful mariners
  The social cann shall flow,
Who swept through the deep,
  While the stormy winds did blow.
          While the stormy winds, &c.

Kaaes, Print, Lancaster.

Charles Wilkins Esq.: Barrister/Debtor
Song Sheet

Handwritten song sheet entitled *The Debtor's Song at Lancaster Castle*

Printer: NA

1800s

This item, entitled *The Debtor's Song at Lancaster Castle*, was written by the barrister Charles Wilkins Esq., having been jailed at the Castle for his debts. The song is a sad consideration of the fate of prisoners everywhere, but also speaks of future opportunities and the hope of an eventual release. However, records show no evidence of a Charles Wilkins being committed to the prison, and his sentence and date of incarceration are unknown.

Welcome! Welcome! Brother Debtors
To this poor, but merry, place;
Where there's many a bolt and fetter
Bailiff's dare not show their face
Ne'er despair at your confinement
From your [ ] heart, or your wife,
Wisdom lies in true resignment
Through the varied scenes of life

What was it made Great Alexander
Weep o'er his unhappy fate?
Twas because he could not wander
B'yond this world's strong prison gate

Every island's but a prison
Strongly guarded by the sea;
Kings and princes for this reason
Prisoners are as [ ] we

Though our plaintiffs they are spiteful
And detain our bodies here
Count of day now will soon be over
Then, my boys, we've nought to fear

Typographic Interlude
Old Faces & Transitional Faces

Up until the mid-eighteenth century, European typefaces had characteristics that where derived from the earlier features of the written word and the pen. The features of these so-called Old Faces included letterforms with an inclined axis (also described as 'stress'), low contrast between thick and thin strokes, and a 'humanistic' form that was influenced by the letterforms found in early manuscripts.[10] Many of the typefaces used in Britain were of Dutch origin, and although Dutch type designers such as Christoffel Van Dijck (1605–1670) and Dirk Voskens (1647–1691) were considered masters of the typographic art, the employment of their typefaces by British type founders and printers was often poor.[10] The introduction of

Old Face (1659)

Old Face (1710)

strict censorship laws[†] and restrictions on which publishers could trade, also stifled the development of native printing and typography.

In 1667 the reliance on imported type was loosened by the employment at the Oxford University Press of Dutch type founder, Peter de Walpergen. De Walpergen, under the patronage of Bishop John Fell (1625–1686), was responsible for some of the first Old Faces to be cast in Britain (the Fell Types),[‡] but British printing remained heavily influenced by the Dutch tradition.[14]

It was not until William Caslon's (1692–1766) intervention into British typefounding and the release of his Roman typeface in 1734,[♩] that the reliance on Dutch type ended.[2] Caslon's expertly constructed typefaces (themselves influenced by the Fell types) helped

Caslon Roman (1734)

---

† The Star Chamber Decree of 1637 and the Licensing Order of 1643, censored publications and restricted the number of publishers permitted to trade. [22]

‡ Bishop John Fell (1625–86), Dean of Christ Church and Vice-Chancellor of the University of Oxford, travelled to the Netherlands (c.1667) and obtained type punches and matrices (the Fell Types) to be used by the Oxford University Press, and was instrumental in the engagement of the Dutchman, Peter de Walpergen.[12]

♩ Caslon's type foundry was established in 1720 but it was not until 1734 that his specimen sheet of typefaces was released to reveal the results of his fourteen years of type development.[29]

to invigorate the British type and print trade, and were used extensively for book and jobbing printing in Britain and abroad. In 1776 the United States Declaration of Independence was set in Caslon's typefaces.[29]

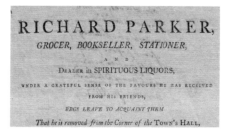

Baskerville Roman (1757)

When in 1757 John Baskerville (1706–1775) of Birmingham produced his Baskerville typeface, along with great innovations in ink and paper, British typography began to enter a new phase. Baskerville's typeface ('stout', with fine lines and enhanced contrast between the thick and thin strokes) not only had a significant influence on type development,[29] but indicates a transition between the Old Faces and the truly Modern Faces (as devised by the Didot and Bodoni foundries) that were to follow. The humanistic features

Bodoni (1818)

of the Old Faces gave way to the more engineered characteristics of the Transitionals, which included increasingly vertical stress and greater stroke contrast.[10] Further advances in printing, ink and paper technologies also allowed the finer details of these typefaces to be realised. That several other foundries quickly copied, adapted and distributed the typefaces of both Caslon and Baskerville, and that these typefaces were used extensively for both book and jobbing

printing, is indicative of their impact.

In our ephemera examples, Richard Parker's advertisement of 1797 (p.26) appears to use a form of the Baskerville typeface for much of its principle lettering, while the publication concerning John Fenton Cawthorne's court martial (1795, p.33), and the 'Hucksters or Higglers' handbill (1796, p.29), both utilise Caslon's typeface (or a derivative of it).

During the nineteenth century the popularity of Old, Transitional and Modern typefaces waxed and waned, with Moderns coming to dominate much of the book printing trade in the mid-1800s, only to see a revival of some Old and Transitionals in the later decades.[17] The development of new typographical forms provided an increasing range of typefaces, but the Old Faces and the Transitionals continued to find favour amongst designers and printers.

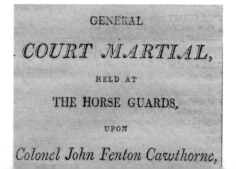

RICHARD PARKER,
GROCER, BOOKSELLER, STATIONER,
A N D
DEALER in SPIRITUOUS LIQUORS,
UNDER A GRATEFUL SENSE OF THE FAVOURS HE HAS RECEIVED
FROM HIS FRIENDS,
BEGS LEAVE TO ACQUAINT THEM
That he is removed from the Corner of the Town's HALL,

GENERAL

COURT MARTIAL,

HELD AT

THE HORSE GUARDS,

UPON

Colonel John Fenton Cawthorne,

This handbill was produced in 1818 during the election for Lancaster's Parliamentary seats. Its author, John Fenton Cawthorne (1753—1831), complains to the Freemen (those landowners who were entitled to vote) of the Borough of Lancaster of an unspoken agreement between his opponents to deny him the election. The final result saw Cawthorne lose on this occasion to John Gladstone and Gabriel Doveton, who between them took the town's two seats. Though defeated in this attempt, Cawthorne, who had been successful in 1812, was returned to the seat in 1820, and again in 1824.[41]

Despite his social status and his political successes, Cawthorne found himself in financial difficulties. His neighbour, David Cragg, with whom he had a long-running dispute, reported with some pleasure that 'Cawthorne the tyrant of his neighbourhood has mostly this summer been kept a prisoner in his own house he not daring to stir out for fear of Bailiffs'.[15]

John Fenton Cawthorne died in 1831. With mounting debts and having no heir, his estate was auctioned off. His town house on Meeting House Lane survived until 1926 when it was demolished to make way for the building of the new Post Office. Only the grand palladian portico survived. It was dismantled and relocated to the back of the nearby Storey Institute on Castle Hill.

Parliamentary Election, 1818: State of the 6th Day's Poll
Public Notice

TO THE
Worthy and Independent
FREEMEN
OF THE
BOROUGH OF *LANCASTER*.

GENTLEMEN,

I did not intend to Address you during this Contest, until your Exertions had placed me above the only Candidate with whom I have contended, and the only one with whom I expected to have to contend.

The unexpected Occurrences of Yesterday and To-day, will have convinced you, that though no Coalition exists between my Opponents, yet that a secret Understanding and Co-operation does exist, and has existed, amongst some of the Members of the Committees of those Gentlemen. I rejoice to find that their Efforts have only been able to place me in a Minority of ONE. I am not dismayed by this slight, and I trust temporary Success, of dishonorable Measures; I pledge myself to maintain the POLL until the last Moment allowed by Law, and call upon you to prove by your Votes, that the time is not yet come, when the Price of this Borough can be calculated, or the Rights of its Freemen invaded with Impunity.

I am, Gentlemen,

Your faithful Servant,

J. F. CAWTHORNE.

Lancaster, 26*th June,* 1818.

State of the 6th Day's Poll.

For Mr. CAWTHORNE........ 990

.... *Gen.* DOVETON............... 991

.... *Mr.* GLADSTONE 1728

Jackson, Printer Lancaster.

September 6, 1814

nhabitants of Lancaster, imm

expressing, at the present

e Seditious and Mischievous

aringly maintained, and are

, do request you, Sir, to cc

ABITANTS of this TOW

Purpose of declaring the

ent to the envied Constitu

bination to resist, to the

es of such visionary Inn

This public notice of 1819 is contemporary with the events of the Peterloo Massacre in Manchester in August of that year. It was a period of great unrest and agitation amongst the general populace who demanded improved economic conditions and parliamentary reform. After the events of Peterloo, Henry Hunt (1773–1835) and other leaders of the protest were briefly incarcerated in Lancaster Castle and charged with seditious conspiracy, before being sent to York Assizes for trial.[27]

The issuing of this handbill in the weeks following Peterloo, indicates the concern felt by the signatories—which included prominent members of the landowning and mercantile classes—about the political situation. It was a rallying call to their supporters and a clear warning to those who might agitate for reform and the radical cause.

Public notice relating to the aftermath of the events of the Peterloo Massacre in Manchester.

Printer: W. Minshull

1819

Seditious and Mischievous Doctrines
Public Notice

Crisis, our Abhorrence of the Seditious and Mischievous Doctrines which have been lately so daringly maintained, and are now actively disseminated in this County, do request you, Sir, to convene an early MEETING of the INHABITANTS of this TOWN and NEIGHBOURHOOD, for the Purpose of declaring their Fidelity to the King;—their Attachment to the envied Constitution of this Realm;—and their firm Determination to resist, to the utmost in their Power, the nefarious Attempts of such visionary Innovators and Disturbers of the Public Peace.

Rd. Atkinson,
Wm. Hinde,
J. F. Cawthorne,
John Dowbiggin,
John Bradshaw,
Joshua Hinde,
Thomas Giles,
Thos. Bowes,
John Manby,

S. Moore,
J. Rowley,
J. B. Nottage,
Strethill Harrison,
Sam. Gregson,
Richd. Atkinson, jun.
Alex. Andrade,
John Higgin, jun.
J. T. Wilson,

J. Booth,
Rob. Housman,
John Gathorne,
John Higgin,
John Armstrong,
Tho. Crook,

Thos. Mason,
Wm. Swainson,
Wm. Sharp,
Wm. Housman,
James Lodge.

To the Worshipful the Mayor of Lancaster.

In Compliance with the above REQUISITION, I do hereby appoint a MEETING of the INHABITANTS of this TOWN and NEIGHBOURHOOD, to be held at the TOWN-HALL, on MONDAY the 13th Instant, at TWELVE o'Clock, for the above Purpose.

T. W. SALISBURY,
Mayor.

SEPTEMBER 8, 1819.

Printed by W. MINSHULL, Great John-Street, Friarage, Lancaster.

Jonathan Binns' Map of Lancaster
Map

Binns' map of Lancaster

Printer: Unknown

1821

There have been a number of noted maps of Lancaster, among them those by: John Speed (1610), Kenneth Docton (1684), Stephen Mackreth (1778), Christopher Clark (1807), Jonathan Binns (1821), Edward Baines (1824), The Ordnance Survey (1844–1845) and that of Harrison and Hall (1877).[19]

The map which Binns (1785–1871), a land surveyor, produced in 1821[31] is particularly interesting, detailed and beautiful. It shows considerable change occurring since the features shown in the maps of Clark and Mackreth. There is an expansion of new streets in several parts of the town, and further industrialisation around the Quay and in the area known as Green Ayre. New churches appear, the town gains a workhouse, and there is redevelopment of the Castle as Lancaster's importance as the judicial centre for the region is cemented. Yet here, the frozen nature of maps is revealed, as these changes belie the beginning of a period of severe economic stagnation that was soon to follow. This included the closure of local banks, leading to a dearth of credit, along with the contraction of the port in the face of competition from Liverpool.[31]

48

S K E R T
. from KENDAL

Captains Row

KIRK LANE

CROSS STREET

Ancient
Ship Yard

Spire of
Sterton Church

ter to Kendal

L

U

NEW BRIDGE

H E G R E E

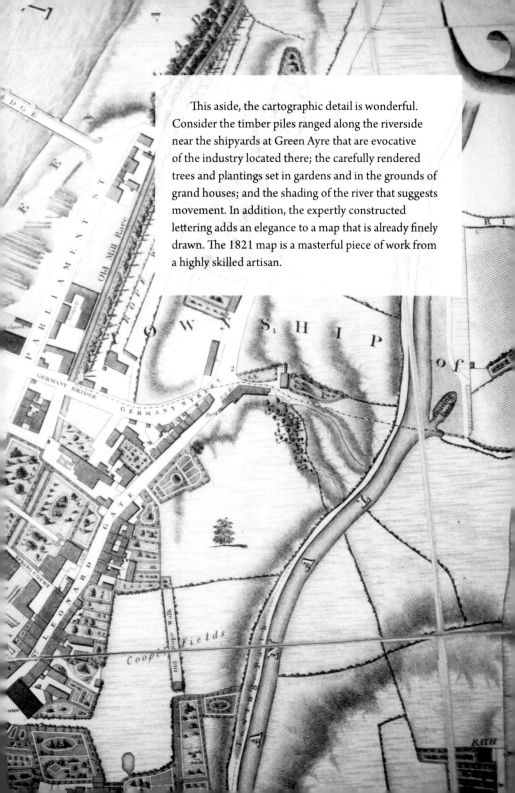

This aside, the cartographic detail is wonderful. Consider the timber piles ranged along the riverside near the shipyards at Green Ayre that are evocative of the industry located there; the carefully rendered trees and plantings set in gardens and in the grounds of grand houses; and the shading of the river that suggests movement. In addition, the expertly constructed lettering adds an elegance to a map that is already finely drawn. The 1821 map is a masterful piece of work from a highly skilled artisan.

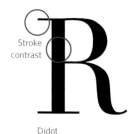

Stroke
contrast

Didot

Unbracketed
serif

Bodoni

Baskerville

Didone

Moderns, also known as Didones, were developed towards the end of the eighteenth century when the increasing contrast between the thick and thin strokes of letters that began with John Baskerville's (1706–1775) typefaces, was taken to a much greater extreme with these new letterforms.

The first typeface that can truly be called a Modern is considered to have been created by the French punchcutter, Firmin Didot (1764–1836) in 1784. This was followed in 1798 by typefaces of the Italian type designer and printer, Giambattista Bodoni (1740–1813), who was heavily influenced by Baskerville's typefaces and studied the typography of Firmin Didot (1764–1836) and Pierre Fournier (1712–1768).[12]

The resulting Moderns are characterised by vertical stress, a somewhat geometric construction and serifs that are typically flat, unbracketed and hairline. They work best when used for titles and at larger point sizes; being generally unsuitable for body text as the high contrast and vertical stress tend to make reading extended lines of letters difficult. In truth, some early examples of Moderns have characteristics not unlike the preceding Transitional typefaces, and distinguishing between these late Transitionals and some Moderns can be difficult.

In our Lancaster ephemera there are many examples of Moderns. Some of the earliest are found on handbills such as that prescribing against 'seditious and mischievous doctrines' (1819, p.44), and the example from the election of 1818 (p.43). A little later we have the deed for the establishment of the Lancaster Banking Company (1826, p.56), followed by the oration from the opening of the Oddfelllows Hall in 1844 (p.72), where they appear in a line of relatively small type (JOHN ARMSTRONG, ESQ.). As late as 1885 they are seen on the Shrievalty document (p.98) in the subtitle, THE HIGH SHERIFF'S.

Though varied in their design, all of these examples have characteristics indicative of the Moderns. Their use throughout much of the nineteenth century shows their value to the print trade, particularly when used for titling.

Fat Faces

As the expanding economy of the early nineteenth century became increasingly dominated by commerce, advertisements began to utilise the newly developed Fat Face. These letterforms were in effect, exaggerated versions of the Modern. Their engorged stems and strokes and the extreme contrast between thick and thin stokes, were ideal for catching the eye.

Robert Thorne (1754–1820) is generally credited with the design of the first Fat Face sometime around 1810,[17] with other foundries quickly developing their own (often copying or modifying those of their competitors) for use on posters, advertisements and handbills.

CAWTHORNE.

Election results, 1818 (p.43)

SALISBURY,

Seditious & mischievous doctrines, 1819 (p.44)

SHERIFF'S

Shrievalty proceedings, 1885 (p.98)

Broadside ballad, 1826 (p.61)

The Fat Face is a typographic request to 'look at me!'

In Lancaster, we find some early examples of Fat Faces on the handbills and broadsides associated with events such as elections, public executions and political proclamations; indicative of their use beyond commerce. The election handbill of 1818 (p.42), containing the word FREEMEN, being the earliest of these. Other examples appear during the following decades, and here the difference between Moderns and Fat Faces is sometimes less distinct and more about degrees of stroke contrast and stroke width. Examples are found on the 1826 broadsides for the Winton Murder (p.61), the sentencing handbill of 1827 (p.62), and the *The Radicals Wonderful Six!!!* broadside ballad (1826, p.68). From 1859 we have both the Chartist poster (p.80) and a sans serif example of a Fat Face from the notice concerning cattle at Skerton (p.86).

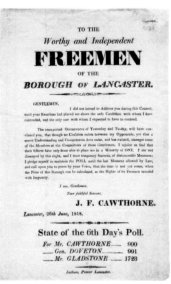

Handbill, 1818, (p.42)

Broadside ballad,
mid-1800s, (p.68)

An interesting example of the diversity of these letterforms is shown in the Chartist poster. Here we find three variations on the Fat Face: BOROUGH ELECTION; SHADES (a slab-serif); and A MANIFESTO, which has an unusual condensed and elongated form.

The widespread use of Fat Faces in Britain declined towards the middle and later part of the nineteenth century when they were superseded by an increasing range of other letterforms, amongst them a plethora of Ornamented tyepfaces.[17] This change in typographic use is also seen in our Lancaster ephemera, although the use of Moderns appears to persist here for some time.

A popular revival of the Fat Face did occur in the early twentieth century, with foundries such as American Type Founders developing Ultra Bodoni (1928), and Stephenson Blake offering the typeface known as Thorowgood (inherited from Stephenson Blake's incorporation of Thorne's Fann Street type foundry in 1820). More recently, digital type foundries have reinterpreted and released new Fat Faces (e.g. Surveyor by Hoefler and Frere-Jones, 2014) as designers look to utilise these striking and attention-grabbing letterforms.

Chartist poster, 1859 (p.80)

Broadside ballad, 1826, (p.60)

DEED

FOR ESTABLISHING

THE

LANCASTER

BANKING COMPANY.

DATED 20th SEPTEMBER, 1826.

LANCASTER:

PRINTED BY HOLME & JACKSON, NEW-STREET.

M.DCCC.XXXI.

The Lancaster Banking Company was formed in September 1826 in response to the collapse of two local banks: Thomas Worswick Sons & Company, and Dilworth, Arthington & Birkett.[31] This deed of 20th September 1826 establishes the founding of the new company. Several prominent Lancastrians acted as directors for the new bank, including Leonard Redmayne (a director of Gillow & Co.), Thomas Storey (founder of the Storey Institute, b.1825) and Charles Blades (Mayor, 1871–1872). The first manager, John Coulston, was to remain in his post for forty years.[34]

In 1869 the company commissioned architects Austin and Paley to design their central branch on Church Street.[26] The building, created in the Italian palazzo style, has a wealth of classical architectural features that includes a modillion cornice, Corinthian pilasters and an entablature with carved acanthus leaves. The renowned Lancaster firm of Gillow & Co. were to provide its fine furnishings.

In October 1907 the bank was amalgamated with the Manchester and Liverpool District Banking Company (est. 1829), resulting in the end of locally established banks in the area. In 1970 the company was incorporated into the National Westminster Bank.[34]

Cover of the *Deed for Establishing the Lancaster Banking Company*

Printer: Holme & Jackson

1826

Deed for Establishing the Lancaster Banking Company Deed

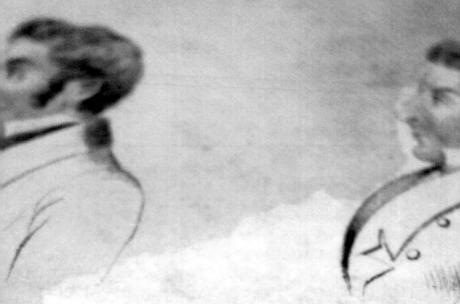

MC KEAND.

MICHAEL MC. KE.

MRS. BRANES.

Trial of the McKean Brothers
Trial Transcript

The trial of the McKean brothers in 1826 for the murder of Elizabeth Bate at the Jolly Carter pub at Winton in Cheshire, was well publicised in Lancaster and beyond. In addition to the printing of a broadside about the event, the entire transcript of the trial was reproduced as a book. It seems a curiously modern publication that includes not only portraits of those involved, but details of the public house where the events occurred, including the highlighting of a 'remarkable stain' formed by the blood of the victim. Its various sensational elements would not be out of place in a modern tabloid newspaper, and the sketches of the people are not unlike those seen today, as artists try to provide representations of those appearing at trials. It is both a fascinating insight into the legal process at the time, and a disturbing reminder of people's curiosity at the plight of others.

Illustrations from the transcript of the trial of the McKean brothers (left), the cover of the publication (bottom left), and the 'remarkable stain' mentioned during the trial (bottom right)

Printer: Pratt, Manchester

1826

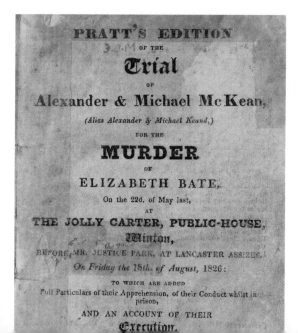

PRATT'S EDITION
OF THE
Trial
OF
Alexander & Michael McKean,
(*Alias Alexander & Michael Keand,*)
FOR THE
MURDER
OF
ELIZABETH BATE,
On the 22d. of May last,
AT
THE JOLLY CARTER, PUBLIC-HOUSE,
Winton,
BEFORE MR. JUSTICE PARK, AT LANCASTER ASSIZES,
On Friday the 18th. of August, 1826:
TO WHICH ARE ADDED
Full Particulars of their Apprehension, of their Conduct whilst in prison,
AND AN ACCOUNT OF THEIR
Execution.

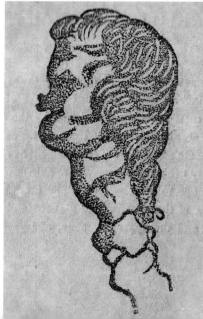

This macabre illustration and its accompanying song relates to the execution of two brothers, Alexander and Michael McKean in August 1826 for murder. The brothers, aged 30 and 25, were staying at the Jolly Carter pub in Winton near Manchester on the evening of May 22nd. The death of their victim, the pub's maid, Elizabeth Bate, appears to have been the result of a bungled robbery. Her cry of 'murder' was stifled as Alexander McKean cut her throat. As she investigated Elizabeth's scream, the landlady, Mrs Blears, was confronted by Michael McKean, who stabbed her before rushing out of the pub. Mrs Blears survived the attack.

The McKeans fled north and in the ensuing manhunt, were eventually captured near Kirby Stephen in Cumbria after a local man spotted their likeness in a wanted poster. The brothers were taken to Lancaster, the site of the assizes court, where they found the streets thronged with people and the air 'filled with hooting and hissing and maledictions against the bloody murderers'. A full transcript of this notorious trial was published to much public interest.

The broadside relates the details of the murder and subsequent chase and trial: broadsides being a popular means to commemorate these events. It's possible that the accompanying illustration was created specifically for the execution, though it's more likely to have been a stock item used for these occasions.

Illustration from the broadside ballad produced to commemorate the execution of the McKean brothers

Printer: Clark
1826

Execution of the McKean Brothers
Broadside Ballad

THE FULL
SENTENCES

Of the Crown Prisoners, confined in his Majest Gaol the Castle of Lancaster, who have taken th trials before Mr. Justice Bayley, at the Assi. commencing on the 29th of August, 1827.

Thomas Seddon, aged 26, and William Davenport, 40, for having burglariously broken and en the dwelling house of Thomas Newton, at Prestwich.—*Death recorded.*

John Schofield, 27, for having stolen, at Birtle-cum-Bamford, a cow.—*Death recorded.*

Jonathan Brookes, 14, and William Adshead, 19, for killing and slaying Charles Barlow, at Man er.—*Brookes fined 1s. and discharged: Adshead imprisoned 3 months.*

William Fay, 19, for having aided and abetted Jonathan Brookes to kill and slay Charles Barlo Manchester.—*Imprisoned one year.*

James Hurst, 23, and John Kemp, 31, for having assaulted Obadiah Marland, on the highw Ashton-under-line, and robbed him of a snuff box, &c.—*Hurst Death*; *Kemp death record*

George Boardman, 29, for killing and slaying James Cooke, at Newton.—*Acquitted*

James Henthorn, 30, Richard Hurst, 50, and Thomas Bottomley, 30, for having burglari broken and entered the dwelling house of John Shaw, at Oldham.—*Death.*

Thomas Connolley, 16, for uttering to Thomas Barlow Jervis, at Manchester, a forged check, f payment of £10, &c.—*Death recorded.*

Thomas Davies, 26, for killing and slaying Daniel Wilde, at Manchester.—*Imprisoned one mo*

Robert Clough, 26, for having burglariously broken into the dwelling house of John Shaw, at ham, and having stolen therein, a Bank of England note for thirty pounds, &c.—*Acquitted.*

George Clough, 22, for breaking into the dwelling house of John Buckley, at Oldham,—*Acqu*

Joseph Shaw, 23, for having broken into the dwelling house of James Scanlan, at Ashton-unde stolen 3 watches, &c.—*Death.*

James Wilkinson, 39, for having stolen, at Manchester, two mares.—*Death.*

John Entwisle, 25, and Mathew Clayton, 23, for having burglariously broken and entere dwelling house of Robert Andrew, at Harpurhey.—*Death recorded.*

Thomas Howarth, 27, for having stolen at Salford, a cow, property of Moses Hardman.—*Deat*

John Coates, 36, David Rowland, 22, and Joseph Adkinson, 21, for having burglariously broke entered the dwelling house of James Cheetham, at Heaton Norris.—*Death recorded.*

William Thornell, 26, and Francis O'Neal, 21, for killing Thomas Aspen, at Manchester.—*Acq*

Jonathan Howarth, 23, George Howarth, 53, George Howarth, 25, for killing and slaying Thompson, at Manchester.—*Imprisoned 2 months each.*

Thomas Hays, 19, and Thomas Partington, 29, for killing and slaying Thomas Clough, at Sa Heys imprisoned 3 calendar months, Partington 6 months.

Robert Allen, 22, for having aided and abetted Thomas Heys, to kill and slay Thomas Clou Salford. *Imprisoned 6 months.*

Jeiah Sutton, 21, Patrick Crayton, 23, and Ann Boardman, 47, for having broken into the d house of John Jenkins, at Tonge-with-Haulgh. *Sutton and Crayton Death rec. Boardman*

John Lawton, 22, for stealing, at Chalderton, one heifer, property of Alice Hilton.—*Death r*

John Gordon, 32, for stealing, at Manchester, one gelding, property of John Fielden.—*Death*

Patrick Leary, 22, and John Jones, 20, for highway robbery at Pendleton.—*Death recorded.*

Thomas Whiteley, 40, for having in his possession, at Lancaster, a forged five pound Bank o land note.—*Transported 14 years.*

Elizabeth Dean, 36, and Margaret Parr, 22, for passing bad money, at Eccleston.—*No prosec*

John Matley, 51, for having forged certain certificates, at Manchester, in order to receive c arrears of pension. *Death recorded.*

John Irvin, 37, for forgery, at Manchester. *No Prosecution.*

James Dugdale, 30, for uttering forged Bank of England notes, at Clitheroe. *Acquitted.*

James Leather, 41, for cow stealing.—*Death recorded.*

Thomas Logan, 31, for killing and slaying John Murphy, at Warrington.—*Acquitted.*

James Thompson, 36, for having stolen, at Liverpool, one gelding.—*Death recorded.*

The Full Sentences Handbill

At the time of the publication of this handbill, teams of judges would travel the country presiding over trials at a select number of towns such at Lancaster. No more than a flimsy scrap of tissue-thin paper, this handbill of 1827 is a poignant reminder of the reality of life for people who fell foul of the law.

In addition to those tried by Mr Justice Bayley and sentenced to death for murder, there were others who would be given the same punishment for far less serious crimes. Amongst them were (ages given in brackets):

Thomas Seddon (26): burglary
William Davenport (40): burglary
John Schofield (27): theft
Thomas Connolley (16): passing forged cheque
James Wilkinson (39): theft of two mares
James Leather (41): theft of a cow

Generations of a family might be similarly sentenced for no more than the theft of handkerchiefs, as in the case of William (60), Roger (23) and George Heyworth (18). For Ann Mason (25), the sentence was death for the theft of a shawl. While for Thomas Whitely (40), perhaps considered fortunate, the sentence was transportation for fourteen years for possessing a forged banknote. Death sentences were sometimes commuted, but the harshness of the law at this time is apparent.

Handbill detailing sentences given to offenders appearing at the Lancaster Assizes on 29th August, 1827

Printer: Bell
1827

63

Municipal Boundary and Division into Wards of the Borough of Lancaster
Report with map

Map of the Municipal Boundary and Division into Wards of the Borough of Lancaster

Printer: Unknown

1831

This map is included in a report into the proposed reorganisation of the municipal and political boundaries of the Borough of Lancaster. These changes, which placed the area of Skerton to the north under the control of the Municipal Committee and divided the town into three main wards, acted to shape the political geography of the town. One striking feature is the size of Lancaster at this time; it being so much smaller than its current boundaries that now stretch to incorporate the once separate township of Scotforth in the south, along with areas such a Greaves, Bowerham and Hala that emerged later.

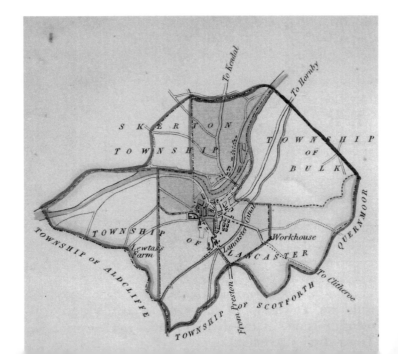

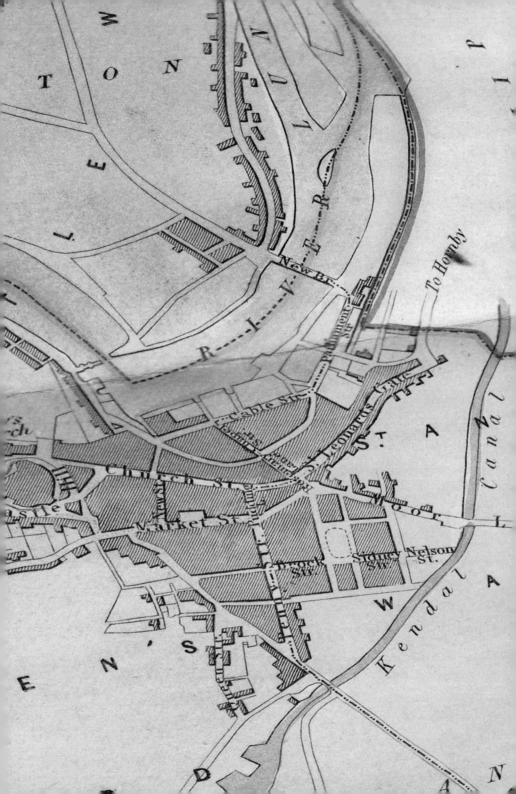

Insane Persons Lunatics and Idiots.

In-door Out-door Asylum Vouchers

Males Females Males Females Males Females

Classes of Pauper at the Lancaster Union Workhouse Report

The Lancaster Union Workhouse was established in 1788 and located just north of the town on the road to the area known as Quernmore. In 1831 the newly formed Lancaster Poor Law Union took over the running of the workhouse.[40]

The Poor Law Amendment Act of 1834 created a more centrally enforced system based on the administrative unit of the local Poor Law Union, with eligibility tests aimed to restrict access to Poor Relief.[40] More importantly, the law sought to change the perception of the poor. It considered them responsible for their own situation and able to change it, if only they would choose to do so (a philosophy that some politicians still espouse even today).

The report of 1843 details the financial and social condition of the Workhouse, as well as categorising the inmates into a number of classes that included the infirm, aged, insane, idiots, mothers of illegitimate children, widows, victims of accidents and those suffering from sickness. Yet the common characteristics of all these unfortunates was that they were poor; people who, through poverty, indebtedness, infirmity or unemployment, were unable to support themselves.

After a number of expansions and reorganisations the workhouse was ultimately incorporated into the NHS in 1948. The main workhouse building no longer stands, but parts of the institution survive on the south side of the site on Quernmore Road.

Table taken from a report of the Lancaster Union Workhouse on the classification of paupers who were in receipt of aid at the institution

Printer: W. Ireland

1843

The Radicals Wonderful Six!!!
Broadside Ballad

What is to be made of this unusual broadside ballad
from the mid-1800s? The song of *The Radicals
Wonderful Six!!!* is an intriguing piece of political satire
that uses humour and innuendo to attack a number
of apparently prominent and powerful figures from
the landed gentry, church and mercantile class. Each
stanza refers to one of the six, and although their names
are omitted, its likely that their identities would have
been obvious to the reader. Songs of this type, widely
distributed as broadsides, were a common means of
airing grievances and ridiculing opponents.

> *Stay awhile my good friends while I sing you a song,*
> *If it aint very witty—it aint very long,*
> *'Tis only to "show up" as Wombwell would say,*
> *The Radical Six in a good humoured way.*

The reference to the 'reform act' in the fourth verse
suggests a date around the time of either the 1832 or
1867 legislation. However, it could also relate to earlier
attempts to address the issue of 'rotten boroughs' that
had been undertaken since 1820.

> *Next a sweet cherub comes in the shape of G—e J—n,*
> *Whose virtues, the saints say, bad men turn their backs on!*
> *He vows the reform act with him shall ne'er halt,*
> *Then be his first act to reform his own "Malt".*

The song is probably an ironic reference to 'radical'
local opponents of the reforms, but it is unclear who
the 'Six' were. The full text of the ballad is given in an
appendix for anyone who would like to try and unravel
the identities of the 'Radicals'.

Broadside ballad entitled *The
Radicals Wonderful Six!!!*

Printer: Unknown
Mid-1800s

A NEW SONG.

THE

RADICALS

WONDERFUL SIX!!

good friends, whilst I sing you a song
witty—it ain't very long—
up," as Wombwell would say,
X in a good humoured way.

hair in the "tail of the Lords,"
astound with his acts, not his
who will fathom what's rotten
from a bag of Brow'd Cotton

Public Notice, 1859 (p. 86)

The sans serif typeface (known also as the Grotesque and the Doric) is characterised—perhaps obviously—by not having serifs. Although letterforms of this kind existed in antiquity in the form of stone-cut Etruscan, Latin and Greek lettering, the earliest know example of a printed monoline sans serif is in an architectural proposal submitted by John Soane in 1779.[23] This seems to have been the precursor for the subsequent development of sans serif typefaces, although the process was somewhat intermittent.

In 1816 William Caslon IV (1780–1869) produced a type specimen of a sans serif under the title of 'Two Lines of English Egyptian'. Though the German Schelter & Giesecke Foundry cast the first complete set of sans serifs in 1825,[21] it wasn't until 1832 that a sans serif,

produced in London by Vincent Figgins (1766–1844), was readily available.[2]

Sans serifs were, however, soon to appear extensively in posters, newspapers and magazines as titles and headlines; their clear, bold lines being ideal as display fonts. As commercial advertising became an increasing part of the print trade, sans serifs were used in all forms of jobbing printing.

In the early and mid-twentieth century, sans serifs were to become a central element in the development of Modernist design and new typographic approaches. This was seen most notably in the Bauhaus movement, De Stijl in the Netherlands, and as expounded in Jan Tschichold's (1902–1974) Die Neue Typographie, while influential sans serif typefaces emerged from designers such as Edward Johnston (Johnston Sans:1916), Paul Renner (Futura:1927), and a little later, Max Miedinger and Eduard Hoffmann, whose Helvetica (originally called Neue Haas Grotesk:1957) has now become one of the most widely used typefaces. The development of elegant sans serif typefaces with a wide range of font weights would enable designers to explore their use in creating print

Advertisement, 1902 (p.116)

LANCASTER

publications that were often both beautiful and experimental.

The earliest example in our Lancaster ephemera occurs as an engraved letterform on the district map of 1831 (p.64). Later, we find large letters on a public notice of 1859 concerning cattle found on the highway (p.86). This example was printed using wooden letterpress that was commonly employed to provide large notices and proclamations. In the handbill for the 1844 inauguration of the Oddfellows Hall (p.72), we see the first metal typeset example (rather than those engraved or made using large wooden letterpress) of a sans serif in the form of an outlined letterform. In our examples from the later part of the nineteenth century we also find hand-drawn sans serifs, such as the engraved letters on the map of the River Lune survey (1891, p.100), as well as an increased use of typeset lettering, like those seen in periodicals (1893, p.104).

Most of the sans serifs found in our ephemera collection are in the form of display faces and titles, while the body text is usually set in serifs. The serif continued to be the typeface of choice for most reading text during the nineteenth century, reflecting the wider

Handbill, 1844 (p.72)

availability of these typefaces in the necessary small point sizes at this time.

In the early part of the twentieth century we encounter a wider variety of examples, including those found on the auctioneer's catalogue (1903, p.119), and others, such as that seen on a car manufacturer's advertisement, that are elegant, condensed and business-like (1902, p.116). The Palatine Hall poster of 1900 (p.114) also uses a number of sans serifs in different sizes and styles, including condensed and bold types. These are combined with an eye-catching large, elongated slab serif.

The later examples in our collection are mainly hand-drawn, including the item for Storey Brothers (1935, p.130) that reflects the Art Deco influences of the time, as well as posters advertising an independent record outlet (1978, p.134), the Dukes Theatre (1983, p.136) and the Musician's Co-operative (1985, p.138).

While the sans serif may appear to be a much simpler version of its serif cousin, the variety of its design and the extent of its use, is considerable.

Y

Poster, 1900 (p.114)

RECORDS

District map, 1831 (p.64)

Poster, 1978 (p.134)

Q U E E N'S

AN ADDRESS,

WRITTEN BY

W. SANDERSON,

ON THE

OPENING OF THE NEW ODDFELLOWS' HALL,

AT LANCASTER,

On Wednesday, the 24th July, 1844,

ON WHICH OCCASION

A PUBLIC DINNER TOOK PLACE,

PRESIDENT:

Dr. D. De Vitre, the Mayor;

VICE-PRESIDENT:

JOHN ARMSTRONG, ESQUIRE.

MANY and various are each thought and plan,
By which man seeks to aid his fellow man;
To check the ills which mar his social life,
And join in love those now in factious strife.
Some to this end go forth God's word to preach,
And midst all dangers holy truths to teach;
Braving the billows of the madd'ning main,
They leave their homes they ne'er may see again;
Wand'ring midst tribes more savage than the storm,
Dauntless to death on what they must perform:
The cross of Christ they on their shoulders bear,
Alike its triumphs and its pains to share.
Some unto Nature's workings turn the mind,
Tracing, through all, that good alone's design'd—
These tell us how with each revolving year,
The changing seasons with their fruits appear;
That though we view with pride the summer's rose,
An equal wisdom made the winter's snows.
Others make Science all their studious care,
Tell what the depths of earth and ocean bear—
Such point to man how all is for his use,
His *use*—my friends—but not for his *abuse*.
Thus in this changeless world, though ever new,
Do various men their various plans pursue;
And as each one, whatever be his part,
May good perform if good be in his heart,
Unto your minds allow me to recall
The wish of those who built this spacious Hall:
They, though they own themselves a humble band,
Would for man's good fain stretch a helping hand;
As Brothers join'd, would aid a Brother's lot,
And chase disease far from his low-roof'd cot;
Then should unto his previous happy home
The blighting hand of with'ring sickness come,
Arm'd with the dread all-conqu'ring arm of death,
They fain would soothe his last, his parting breath;
And, when no more, they his remains would save
From the sad rites which mark a pauper's grave!
So that his friends, as they a tear-drop paid,
Might see them plac'd where his forefathers' laid.
That unto such may still be greater power
Of yielding succour in each needy hour,
And bringing solace unto him in pain,
This Hall is built—'tis hop'd not built in vain.
O! may it be by GOD's protecting hand,
Another boon hence added to our land;
Based on His word, which has for ages stood,
May it, through *that*, in aim and end be good.

WATKINSON, PRINTER, SUN-STREET, LANCASTER.

The Oddfellows were a benevolent society that was established in England in the late 1700s. In Lancaster, their benefits and activities included a widows and orphans fund, sickness insurance and annual festivities organised for members and supporters.

In 1844 three lodges collaborated to erect a new hall on Brock Street as a place for meeting and entertainment. It was opened in July of that year by a parade of 800 society members carrying banners and accompanied by a band. The procession marched to the Priory on Castle Hill and then back to the hall for a celebratory dinner.[16]

A dinner address was written to commemorate the event. Its author, William Sanderson (1804–1848), was a local writer, poet and 'some-time contributor to the *Lancaster Gazette*'.[11] Two years earlier he had written a poem for a dinner held at the Assembly Rooms on King Street that was given in honour for the distinguished Lancaster scientists, Dr. William Whewell (1794–1866) and Sir Richard Owen (1804–1892). William Sanderson published a number of poetical works before his death in 1848, including the collection entitled *Songs and Miscellaneous Poems*.[11]

Dinner address by William Sanderson to commemorate the opening of the new Oddfellows Hall

Printer: Watkinson

1844

On the Opening of the New Oddfellows Hall
Handbill

73

Ecclesiastical Architecture: Decorated Windows Pamphlet

Edmund Sharpe (1809–1872) was one of Lancaster's most important and talented architects. Along with his business partners at Austin, Paley and Sharpe, Edmund was responsible for many of the city's most beautiful and iconic buildings, including: the Storey Institute, the Royal Lancaster Infirmary, the Militia Barracks and the Co-operative Society's New Street store.[26] There are few parts of Lancaster that do not have the mark of these hugely influential designers on them.

This illustration is taken from Sharpe's publication *Ecclesiastic Architecture: Decorated Windows*, in which he traced the development of these architectural features through a series of examples taken from buildings that included: Exeter Cathedral, Cartmel Abbey (Cumbria) and Milton Abbey (Dorset). It not only shows his interest in architectural history but his skill as an artist.

Illustration taken from *Ecclesiastical Architecture: Decorated Windows* by Edmund Sharpe

Printer: Jan Van Voorst, London
1845

The great expanse of Morecambe Bay has long influenced the natural and social conditions of the area that surrounds it. Affecting weather patterns, industry and the connectivity between communities, the wide sands and rushing tides have been a feature that the local inhabitants have long had to adapt to.

In the mid-1800s, coaches would regularly cross the sands, using the tidal interludes to significantly cut the travel time between the towns. However, the journey could be hazardous and there were incidents of coaches becoming stuck or lost in the perilous shifting sands, and deaths were not uncommon for those caught out by the tide.[48] The drama and beauty of the bay crossing has been captured by a number of artists, including William Turner, whose painting *Lancaster Sands* (c.1826) depicts a coach struggling to make progress as the tide begins to rise.

This poster of September 1848 gives the timetable for the coaching service between Ulverston and Lancaster, accompanied by a wonderful illustration of a fully-laden coach moving at full speed. At each end of the route where inns at which travellers might find food and a bed.

The coming of the railway to the area in 1857 effectively saw the end of the over sands coach route across the bay.[31]

Poster advertising the over sands coach service between Ulverston and Lancaster

Printer: J. Jackson, Ulverston
1848

Over Sands Coaches
Poster/Timetable

TIMES OF DEPARTURE OF THE
OVER SANDS
COACHES,
FOR THE MONTH OF SEPTEMBER, 1848,

Between ULVERSTON & LANCASTER.

Lancaster to Ulverston. SEPTEMBER.		H. M.		Ulverston to Lancaster. SEPTEMBER.		H. M.
Friday	1st	7 30 a m		Friday	1st	6 30 a m
Saturday	2nd	8 0 a m		Saturday	2nd	7 0 a m
Monday	4th	9 0 a m		Monday	4th	8 0 a m
Tuesday	5th	9 30 a m		Tuesday	5th	9 0 a m
Wednesday	6th	10 50 a m		Wednesday	6th	9 0 a m
Thursday	7th	10 30 a m		Thursday	7th	11 0 a m
Friday	8th	11 0 a m		Friday	8th	11 30 a m
Saturday	9th	1 30 p m		Saturday	9th	1 0 p m
Monday	11th	2 0 p m		Monday	11th	2 30 p m
Tuesday	12th	3 0 p m		Tuesday	12th	5 0 p m
Wednesday	13th	3 30 p m		Wednesday	13th	5 30 a m
Thursday	14th	4 0 p m		Thursday	14th	6 0 a m
Friday	15th	6 30 a m		Friday	15th	6 0 a m
Saturday	16th	7 0 a m		Saturday	16th	6 30 a m
Monday	18th	8 0 a m		Monday	18th	6 30 a m
Tuesday	19th	9 0 a m		Tuesday	19th	7 30 a m
Wednesday	20th	10 30 a m		Wednesday	20th	9 0 a m
Thursday	21st	10 30 a m		Thursday	21st	10 0 a m
Friday	22nd	1 30 p m		Friday	22nd	11 30 a m
Saturday	23rd	1 30 p m		Saturday	23rd	1 0 p m
Monday	25th	2 30 p m		Monday	25th	2 30 p m
Tuesday	26th	3 0 p m		Tuesday	26th	6 0 a m
Wednesday	27th	6 0 a m		Wednesday	27th	6 30 a m
Thursday	28th	6 30 a m		Thursday	28th	6 0 a m
Friday	29th	7 0 a m		Friday	29th	6 30 a m
Saturday	30th	7 30 a m		Saturday	30th	6 30 a m

The Coaches will arrive at the Hest Bank Station in 2 hours after leaving Ulverston.

PLACES OF DEPARTURE:

LANCASTER..KING'S ARMS INN, AND BEAR AND STAFF INN.—ULVERSTON..SUN INN, AND BRADDYLL'S ARMS.

PROPRIETORS............MESSRS. BLAYLOCK, BUTCHER, & Co.

J. JACKSON, PRINTER, MARKET-PLACE, ULVERSTON.

JOHN CARRUTHERS,
GUANO DEALER,
KING STREET, LANCASTER,

Has great pleasure in submitting the following Analysis of his

CONCENTRATED MANURE,

To the Notice of Farmers and Agriculturalists,

And can confidently assure them, from the proofs afforded by the trials of the late season, that it acts almost as an antidote to the Potato Blight, producing healthy and heavy crops, and materially assists in preventing the ravages of the fly, &c., in Swedes and other Turnips. Wheat, Oats, Barley, and all other Serials are peculiarly benefitted wherever it is applied, and by its use the Farmer may secure abundant and luxuriant crops of Hay, or render of great value, pastures which would otherwise be comparatively worthless, by increasing in a wonderful degree, both the quantity and quality of the Herbage.

"Dunsabank, near Richmond, Yorkshire,
" My dear Sir,   "December 1st., 1858.

"I regret that on account of my health, I was obliged to be in London when my Turnips were drawn from the land—the men say that where your Manure was applied they considered the Turnips the best on the farm. If I had been at home actual weight should have decided the question. I think as far as I have had an opportunity of judging that your Artificial Manure will answer well for the Farmers, but I am afraid the profit will be small to yourself. I shall give you an order for next spring.

"I am, my dear Sir, Your's truly,
" MR. JOHN CARRUTHERS.   "WILLIAM LISTER."

Report by DR. FRANKLAND, on the Concentrated Manure, Manufactured by JOHN CARRUTHERS, King Street, Lancaster.

"St. Bartholomew's Hospital, London, E. C.
" MR. JOHN CARRUTHERS.   April 30th, 1858.

" SIR,—I have analytically examined the sample of Manure which you sent for my inspection, and I beg to report that it consists chiefly of a mixture of organic matters, earthy phosphates, and nitrate of soda. The organic matters are rich in Nitrogen, and are equivalent to 6.17 per cent of Ammonia; the earthy phosphates contain 13 per cent of phosphoric acid, whilst the nitrate of soda is present to the extent of 8.88 per cent.

" This is one of the richest Artificial Manures which I have hitherto examined. It is calculated to produce luxuriant crops of either Grain, Grass, or Bulbs; and it contains the fertilizing ingredients in a form suitable for their gradual assimilation by plants. Its effects will extend, though in a diminishing degree, over several years,—a peculiarity by which it is distinguished from most Artificial Manures at present in the market.

"I am, Sir, Your's truly,   " E. FRANKLAND."

PRESENT PRICES:
Best Peruvian Guano at Market Price. Concentrated Manure £10 per Ton. Nitrate of Soda £20.

John Carruthers, Guano Dealer
Advertisement

After independence from Spain in 1824, Peru
experienced an economic boom as a result of the
extraordinary international demand for guano as an
agricultural fertiliser. The period known as the Guano
Age lasted until the mid-1880s when the development
of other sources of fertiliser, and Peru's loss of its guano
resources to Chile in the War of the Pacific, ended the
boom and ultimately bankrupted Peru's economy.[44]
Merchants such as John Carruthers helped to facilitate
the demand for this resource, making Britain the chief
market for Peruvian guano.

Advertisement taken from
Edmondson's Annual Advertiser

Printer: T. Edmondson
1859

    This advertisement uses the statements of customers
and a Dr. Frankland of St. Bartholomew's Hospital,
London, to testify to the quality and effectiveness of the
fertiliser. It appeared in *Edmondson's Annual Advertiser*
together with times for 'the rising and setting of the
sun and moon; a copious calendar, numerous law and
university terms, eclipses, tables of stamps and taxes
etc.'

LANCASTER
BOROUGH ELECTION

A MANIFESTO

FROM THE

SHADES.

TO THE CHARTISTS OF LANCASTER.

FELLOW MEN,

Don't be hood-winked. **FENWICK** offers you a five pounds Franchise and Vote by Ballot. This won't do. You must squeese him hard and bring him to adopt the *Charter, the whole Charter, and nothing but the Charter,* viz:—

Universal Suffrage, Annual Parliaments, Vote by Ballot. Electoral Districts, Payment of Members, and no Property Qualification.

If Fenwick hesitates to go for all these points, **YOU MUST REJECT HIM,** and turn to the *Black* and *Burly-haired* man of Wray; failing whom, you must turn to *PATRIOTIC JOSEY.* **HE WILL BE YOUR MAN!.** The War-cry must then be

DOWN WITH THE

Aristocracy and the Moneyocracy !!

DEMOCRACY FOR EVER !!!

Hurrah ! for JOSEY and the Charter. *That's the Style.*

Given from the Shades, in this year of grace 1859, on the 5th Month, and the 28th day of the Month.

FERGUS O'CONNOR,

Redivivus.

The Chartist movement of the mid-1800s sought to extend the franchise and further the rights of working people through the demands laid out in their 'People's Charter' of 1838. The resulting petition for change was presented to Parliament in 1839, but rejected out-of-hand by MPs.

In August 1842, following Parliament's rejection of a second Charter petition, a Chartist conference took place in Manchester, followed by wide-spread strikes and public disorder (The Plug Plot Riots). In the subsequent arrest of hundreds of Chartists, fifty-nine were sent for trial at Lancaster Assizes. Under what the Chartists called the 'monster indictment', the accused faced nine counts of inciting riots, uprisings, strikes and other forms of disorder.[8]

Among the accused was Feargus O'Connor (1794–1855), the publisher of the *Northern Star* and a leader of the National Charter Association. Although O'Connor and thirty-two others were found guilty, their sentences were never carried out because of a legal technicality. Chartists elsewhere were less fortunate and many endured heavy prison sentences.[25]

This election poster of 1859 is a rallying call to Lancaster Chartists to remember the ideals of the Chartists Manifesto, and to reject 'Aristocracy and Moneyocracy' in favour of democracy. The final part of the poster reads 'Fergus O'Connor, *Redivivus*' (come back to life). It was the invocation of a radical and inspirational figure, now largely forgotten.

Election poster of the Lancaster Chartists

Printer: Unknown

1859

A Manifesto from the Shades
Poster

81

Bill of sale for the provision of a gravestone and inscription

Richard Fawcett, Marble Merchant
Bill of Sale

In 1838, Richard Fawcett acquired the marble works of Townley and Moore at Skerton. The building was positioned on the north bank of the River Lune. Here water from a spring powered the cutting tools that allowed fine marbles and other stone to be shaped and moulded into a variety of products.

Born in Sedbergh in 1810, Richard Fawcett had originally been a partner in a failed marble works in Nottingham. Expanding the Lancaster business and establishing a reputation for high quality work, Fawcett also became a town councillor, a supporter of the local

Bill of sale for the provision of a gravestone and inscription

Printer: Unknown

1859

Mechanics Institute and a board member of a number of organisations, including the Lancaster Poor Union (the workhouse).

This bill of sale from 1859 relates to the supply of a gravestone with an inscription for the burial of one Ann Moore. The stone was to be erected in the graveyard of the nearby hamlet of Halton. The bill proudly advertises the works' execution of 'superior water power' and uses an extravagantly ornamented Blackletter typeface to represent Fawcett's name, along with an open faced sans serif for the words, MARBLE MILLS. One unique feature of the bill is the appearance of Fawcett's own signature, added to the left of the duty stamp. The stamp is interesting in itself. From the late 1600s, businesses paid a stamp duty on transactions, usually administered by local stamping offices. By the middle of the 1800s this took the form of an adhesive stamp attached to the bill of sale or other documents. This is the origins of the adhesive stamps later used for postage.

Richard Fawcett, marble merchant (c.1870)

By the mid-1860s, Fawcett's political and commercial endeavours reached their high point. In 1863 he began building a beautiful new marble works and showrooms on Parliament Street close to the river and railway line. Designed by Edward Paley (1823–1897) in a Venetian Gothic style, the new premises were constructed with modern steam powered cutting engines to increase the capacity and efficiency of production. The building's wide central stairway was said to be particularly impressive, being made of wrought iron and marble. Shortly after the opening of the new works in 1865, Fawcett's long civic service reached its pinnacle when he was elected as Mayor of Lancaster (1865–1866).

For many years the firm continued to provide products for private, civic and commercial customers, but in 1876, faced with debts of nearly £14,000, it

MARBLE M

La

Messrs Moore Lane

To Richard

ble Work in every Branch of the Business, executed

A Gravestone in Mem

Ann Moore includ

Cutting & Laying dow

Church Yard

Paid Vicars fee

5

6

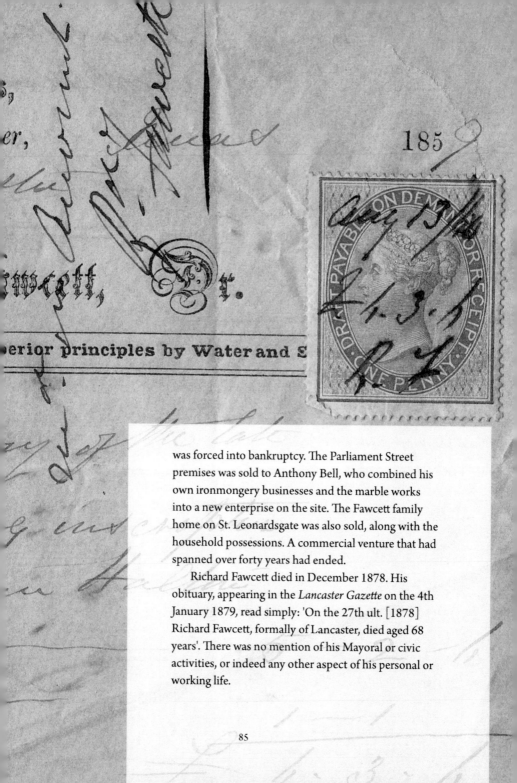

185

erior **principles by Water and S**

was forced into bankruptcy. The Parliament Street premises was sold to Anthony Bell, who combined his own ironmongery businesses and the marble works into a new enterprise on the site. The Fawcett family home on St. Leonardsgate was also sold, along with the household possessions. A commercial venture that had spanned over forty years had ended.

Richard Fawcett died in December 1878. His obituary, appearing in the *Lancaster Gazette* on the 4th January 1879, read simply: 'On the 27th ult. [1878] Richard Fawcett, formally of Lancaster, died aged 68 years'. There was no mention of his Mayoral or civic activities, or indeed any other aspect of his personal or working life.

Persons Causing Cattle to Stand on the Highways at Skerton
Public Notice

It's difficult to know what to make of this notice concerning the offence of allowing cattle to stand on the highways around Skerton ('under the pretence of there being a fair, or market'). It may simply have been designed to prevent the roads being blocked by cattle. However, it may also relate to the passage of traffic across the bridge that was the main link between the township of Skerton on the north bank of the River Lune, with Lancaster to the south. A toll was paid at the bridge's southern end, and presumably cattle left to idle at Skerton—possibly to graze or to be watered at the river—would have restricted not only travel, but the income derived from passage through the toll. The notice, with its large letterpress type, was intended to catch the attention of the public.

NOTICE.

Persons causing Cattle to stand on the Highways at Skerton, so as to obstruct the free passage thereon, (under the pretence of there being a Fair, or Market there) are liable to prosecution, and after this Notice, will be treated as wilful offenders.

Public notice relating to the movement of cattle on the public highways at Skerton

Printer: T. Edmondson

1859

T. PARKER SNOW,

Will deliver a

LECTURE,

ON

The Lost Polar Expediti...

EXPLANATORY OF LIFE IN THE
ARCTIC SEAS

Illustrated by large Diagrams and Sketch...

AND

RELICS FROM THE FRANKLIN EX...

will be exhibited.

To commence at Eight o'...

The Lancaster Athenaeum was established in 1849 when the architect Edmund Sharpe (1809–1872) bought the former Grand Theatre and converted it into a music hall and venue for public lectures. A number of speakers, including the eminent scientists, Richard Owen (1817–1895) and Edmund Wheeler (1804–1892), appeared at the Athenaeum, and the local populace had the opportunity to attend lectures on subjects as diverse as: Fire and its Antagonists, Turkey and the Turks, The Telescope and its Revelations, Nineveh and its Ruins, and The Songs of Robin Hood.

In 1861, Captain William Parker Snow (1817–1895) delivered a lecture entitled The Lost Expedition. The lecture concerned the British polar expedition lead by Sir John Franklin (1786–1847), who, along with his compliment of 128 men, had mysteriously disappeared in 1845 whilst trying to traverse the Northwest Passage.

In 1850, Parker Snow, a former Naval officer, claimed to have had a psychic vision about Franklin's whereabouts and was able to convince the explorer's widow to allow him to take charge of a mission to find her husband. In 1857, after the failure of the initial search, and after several of his own aborted expeditions, Parker Snow was employed by Franklin's widow on a lecture tour designed to finance further attempts at finding the expedition party. When confirmation of the loss of the polar party was eventually made, Parker Snow set about leading a series of attempts to find the expedition's scientific records. Unsuccessful, he ended his final years in New York, writing and lecturing about natural history, exploration and the Franklin Expedition.[28]

Programme for a lecture at the Lancaster Athenaeum on the search for the Franklin Expedition

Printer: T. Edmondson.

1861

The Lost Polar Expedition Programme

This genteel scene of well-dressed couples walking amongst the grounds of an imposing Gothic building, belies the scale of the event of June 1868 that it commemorates: the laying of the foundation stone of the Royal Albert Hospital. Almost 9,000 people attended, with many arriving on special trains from other northern counties. The procession that made its way through the town to the site was followed by a banquet and a concert.[1]

Established by private philanthropy as an institution for young mentally handicapped people, the first patients arrived in December 1870. Numbers rose from an initial sixty-six to nearly six hundred by the turn of the century. At first seeking to educate and rehabilitate patients, the hospital increasingly developed a policy of life-long institutionalisation. This was partly influenced by the belief, held by some in society, that these patients should be segregated from the wider community.[1]

In 1948 the hospital was integrated within the NHS. This removed the need for philanthropic funding and saw an increase in staffing and a relaxation of many of the old rules and regulations. By the 1980s an emphasis on 'community care' for patients with learning difficulties was integral to government mental health policy, with the intention that large institutions such as the Royal Albert should be phased out. In 1996 the Royal Albert closed, its changing care regimes and philosophies reflecting many of the wider changes in society in relation to mental health care.

Cover illustration from the official programme for the laying of the foundation stone of the Royal Albert Asylum

Printer: E & J. T. Milner

1868

Royal Albert Asylum: Laying of the Foundation Stone
Programme

Shrigley and Hunt, Decorative Glassmakers
Advertisement

Right: Advertisement for Shrigley and Hunt in *Milner's Railway Digest*

Printer: Milner 1879

Below: One of a set of ceramic tiles in the entranceway to Shrigley and Hunt's workshops on Castle Park, which includes the company monograph

The firm of Shrigley and Hunt was established in Lancaster in the late 1860s, being an amalgamation of the company of painters, guilders and carvers founded by Joseph Shrigley in Lancaster in 1750, and that of the builder, John Hunt, whose company in Hoddesdon (Herts.) had been trading since 1719.[30] It was John's son, Arthur (1849–1917), who took over the Shrigley enterprise after the death of Arthur Shrigley (–1868), creating a new company that combined the best skills and business contacts of its two component parts.

Offering painting, carving, gilding, stained glass and art tiles, the company gained a reputation for producing work of the highest quality, employing skilled artists such as John Milner Allen, Alex Skirving, Edward Holmes Jewitt and Carl Almquist.[30] In addition to the examples of their work found elsewhere in the country, in Lancaster, stained glass can be seen in Christ Church, St. Peter's Catholic Cathedral and the Priory. Their Lancaster offices and workshop (they also had premises in London) can still be found at Castle Park. Here the faded name of the company is still visible on the façade, and there are some fine examples of their tiles set in the entranceway that carry the company monograph.

The hand-drawn lettering and the figures in this advertisement have the feel of a sketch, as might be drafted for one of their window or tile designs. It is included in an issue of *Milner's Railway Digest*, a local periodical that provided rail and coaching timetables, and the times of the tides on Morecambe Bay—all important information for travellers visiting the area.

VS · LVCAS

CASTLE H
DECORATIVE
ART TILE
PAINTER

RS of CHVRCH

IN AX CELSIS DE

PUBLIC

Know originally as the Egyptian, the slab serif is characterised by blocky, squared-off serifs and often uniform stroke widths. The first examples appeared in Britain around 1815 in a specimen sheet by Vincent Figgins (1766–1844),[2] although Robert Thorne (d.1820) may have been their true originator.[10][13]

Few forms of type have resulted in such strong response from commentators. For Hansard (1825), they were a 'typographical monstrosity', revealing perhaps the shock felt at such radically different letterforms. Almost a hundred years after their inception some were driven to call them 'degenerate'.[3] For others, however, they are outstanding examples of typographic invention, exemplifying the dominant characteristics of the Regency period; a time that seemed 'less concerned with pomposity and frivolity'.[12] Certainly, these letterforms have a sense of solidity to them, and when done well can still be elegant.

There are a number of examples in this ephemera collection. The first is found on the title page of Pratt's 1826 transcript of the trial of the McKean brothers (p.59). We find another on the broadside ballad entitled *The Radicals Wonderful Six!!!* (p.68). The date of this

Handbill, 1844 (p.72)

item is unknown, although some point in the mid-1800s is likely.

In 1844 we find a similar example on the handbill for the opening of the Oddfellows Hall (p.72), though in a considerably smaller font size. A little later there is an example on the Over Sands Coaches poster of 1848 (p.77). Then on a Chartist poster of 1859 (p.80) there are two forms of the slab: a narrow, almost elongated example alongside a shorter, fatter sibling. The Oddfellows and Pratt examples are most likely the typeface *Antique* from Vincent Figgins' foundry and first shown in 1815. Figgins slab serif has been considered by some to be the finest example of its kind of that period.[12] Other foundries soon followed Figgins and Thorne, producing their own versions for use in advertisements and other jobbing printing. As late as 1900 the slab serif is found on the large posters advertising the lectures at Palatine Hall (p.115). Here the style is reminiscent of that found on 'Wild West' posters, with their elongated stems, exaggerated serifs and the turned-up legs on the letter R. The size of the lettering indicates they are wood rather than metal type.

Trial transcript, 1826 (p.59)

The early part of the next century saw the design of a number of widely used slab serifs that included Litho Antique (1910), Memphis (1929), Rockwell (1933) and Stymie (1931). This rash of new typefaces seemed to reflect the increasingly industrialised, modern and rationalist nature of the period. The typewriter face Courier (1955), is a further example of the versatility of this letterform.

Modern typographers have continued to revive and reinterpret these striking letterforms. Popular contemporary examples include Archer (2001) and Museo Slab (2009).

Museo Slab, 2009,
Exlibris Font Foundry

Archer, 2001,
Hoefler & Frere-Jones

Broadside Ballad,
mid-1800s (p.68)

In 1885 the Mechanics Institute—later to become the Storey Institute—held a series of educational talks supported by the Gilchrist Educational Trust. The Trust was founded by Dr. John Borthwick Gilchrist (1759–1841) whose lifelong promotion of popular education contributed to the establishment of the London Mechanics Institute, University College London and the London Oriental Institution. The Gilchrist Educational Trust that resulted from the terms of his will, worked closely with the University Extension Movement and the Workers' Educational Association to increase access to knowledge and learning amongst the wider population.[39]

The popularity of the Gilchrist Lecturers in Lancaster is shown in the committee notes, which record that in addition to the 1,200 people who attended the course of lectures, large numbers were turned away because of over subscription. The figure of 1,200 is remarkable when one considers that the total population of the town was around 16,000 at this point. Admission was one penny and the lecturers included illustrations projected by a magic lantern.

The Mechanics and the Storey Institute that followed, played key educational and cultural roles in the town: being the location of the first public library and having a number of eminent scientists, including William Turner (1832–1916), Edward Frankland (1825–1899), William Whewell (1794–1866) and the noted palaeontologist, Richard Owen (1804–1892), closely associated with them.

Minutes of a Meeting for the Gilchrist Lectures
Minutes

Meetings.
14 — Dec. 18.
Gilchrist Lec
given at Lanea
in 1885.

Supplement to the Lancaster Gazette,

JULY 18th, 1885.

THE SHRIEVALTY

OF

JAMES WILLIAMSON, ESQ., J.P., D.L.,

OF RYELANDS.

A RECORD

OF

THE HIGH SHERIFF'S
STATE ENTRY INTO LANCASTER,

AND OF THE PROCEEDINGS AT

THE PUBLIC BREAKFAST AT RYELANDS,

JULY 11th, 1885.

Printed and Published by W. King, of 16, Chapel Street, Lancaster, at the Office, No. 29, Market Street,

The name of Williamson was inextricably linked with the financial and political development of Lancaster for over a hundred years from the mid-1800s onwards. The wealth that resulted from the development of the Lune Mills linoleum factory in 1844, enabled the Williamsons to build an economic and political dynasty that would result in positions as Mayor, Member of Parliament and Lord High Sheriff of the County (The Shrievalty).

It was in this latter capacity of Lord High Sheriff that James Williamson (1842–1930) held a 'breakfast feast' in the grounds of his town residence of Ryelands House to celebrate his ceremonial arrival to the position.[43] This document of 1885 details the programme of events as well as the menu of the feast that was presented to the guests. In addition to the great and the good of the town, all male adults in Lancaster and the district for ten miles around were invited to the breakfast at Ryelands, with over 10,000 accepting.

This marks the Williamsons approaching the height of their success, with their linoleum factory employing some 2,500 workers (around a fifth of the town's male working population) and with a raft of public buildings only a few years away from being commissioned through their patronage, including the Royal Lancaster Infirmary and the Town Hall.

Supplement to the *Lancaster Gazette* giving a record of the proceedings of the Shrievalty, or Lord High Sheriff of Lancaster's arrival in the town

Printer: W. King

1885

The Shrievalty
Proceedings

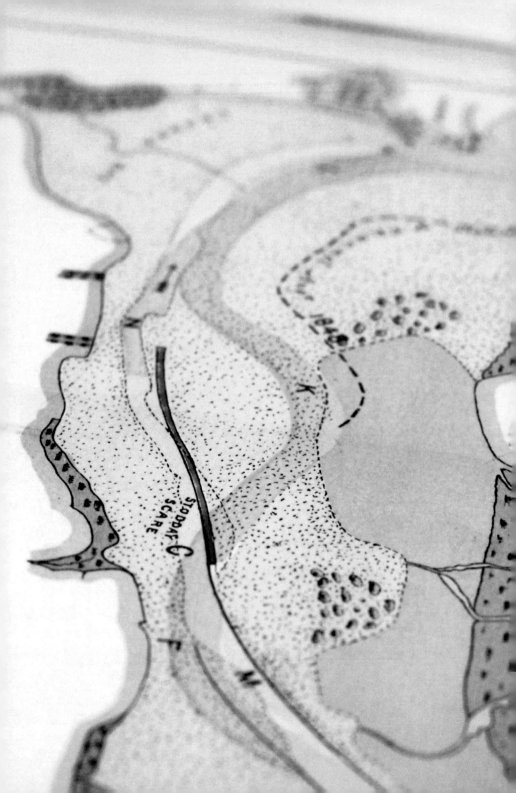

STODDAY
SCARE

River Lune Deep Water Channel
Report and Map

The importance of the River Lune in the development of Lancaster cannot be understated. The river's curving course around the hill that was to be fortified and occupied for over 1,500 years, is the key reason for the town's establishment. Later, it would form the conduit that allowed goods from the West Indies, Africa and the Americas to be brought to Lancaster, and for ships to be built in the yards that developed along its banks. It also allowed furniture, linoleum, clothing and the other products of the emerging industrialism of which the region was so central, to be exported around the world.

This map, drawn by Stevenson of Edinburgh, is part of a report that charted the river's navigable water channel. The report noted that the failure of the Port Commissioners to both maintain the 'training walls' that helped to ensure the channel depth, and to upkeep dredging, was severely endangering the navigability of the river, and consequently the economy of the town. The report concluded that extending the training walls (shown as a red line on the map) and undertaking more dredging was essential if use of the river for commerce was to continue.

Map detailing aspects of the topography of the River Lune from *A Report of the Commissioners of St. George's Quay*, by Messrs D & T Stevenson, Civil Engineers, Edinburgh.

Printer: Unknown

1891

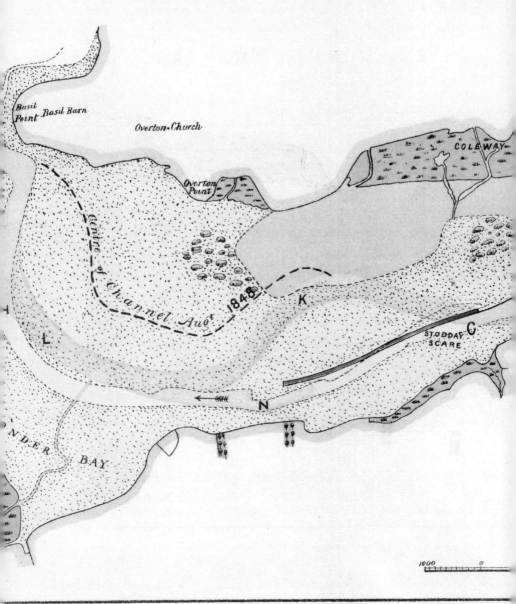

SKETCH PLAN OF RIVER L

Present Deep Water Channel Coloured

Basil
Point Basil Barn

Overton • Church

Overton
Point

COLEWAY

Centre of Channel Aug.ᵗ 1848

K

L

STODDAY
SCARE

C

N

NDER
BAY

1000   0

Lancaster.

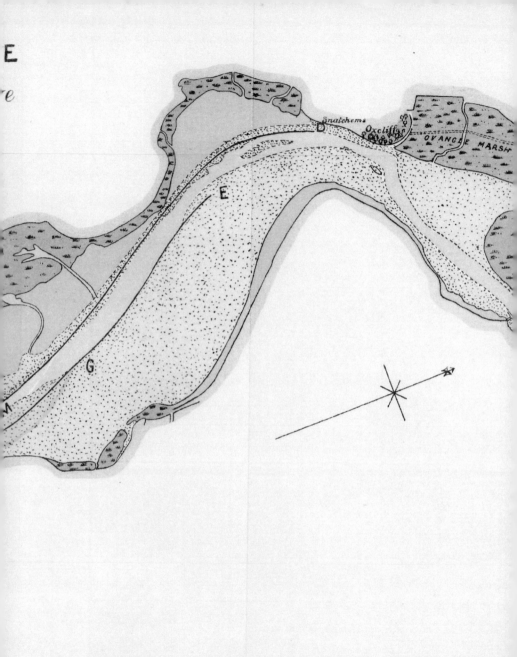

E

re

Snatchems

Oxcliffe

OVANGLE MARSH

E

G

M

2000   3000   4000 Feet

D & T. Ste

Edinbu

Rimmon Clayton & Sons
Advertisement

This illustration of a penny farthing and its occupant appeared in the pages of *The Comet,* a Lancaster periodical of the later 1800s. It is part of an advertisement for Rimmon Clayton & Sons who sold bicycles from their Brock Street Cycle Depot. The cost of bicycles, from between £4 and £20, gives some idea of the luxury nature of these machines, considering that the average weekly wage for a skilled worker at the time was between £1 and £2. The company offered bicycle models that included: the Raglan, New Howe, Quadrant, Crypto and the unnervingly titled, Psycho.

Advertisement from the Lancaster periodical *The Comet*

Printer: Eaton & Bulfield

1893

(Opposite) Plan for the proposed
extension of the Lancaster
Market and the building of a new
hotel

Printer: Eaton & Bulfield
1894

Amongst the interesting aspects of this plan for the redevelopment of Lancaster Market is the beautiful embellishments provided in the curling type of the title (a letterform designed by William Caslon IV). These kinds of ornamented typeface were heavily used during the later half of the nineteenth century as advertising and commercialisation became increasingly common aspects of public life.

There must have been some modification of the original planning proposal because the Black Horse Inn that is shown on the site (and presumably ear-marked for demolition) was still in existence until 1960, when it was removed as part of a much later redevelopment of the Market area.[32] The creation of the new hotel, proposed on the plan alongside the development of the market, was never undertaken. There must have been a number of imagined and hoped for developments at this time that never came to fruition or saw significant change, as competing interests vied for access to land and development opportunities.

(Below) A typeface designed by
William Caslon IV that is used on
the plan

Proposed Market Extension
Development Plan

ORATION OF

KING PLACE

CORN MARKET STREET

MARKET HALL

CORN MARKET

B

Q

GILLSON'S HOSPITAL

SITE OF MARKET EXTENSION

BLACK HORSE INN

M.H. 8'5" DEEP

M.H. 6'0" DEEP

2'0" x 1'8" SEWER

COMMON GARDEN STRE

RUSSELL STREET

9" SEWER

M.H. 8'5" DEEP

WARING'S YARD

SITE OF NEW HOTEL

RILEY'S YARD

This remarkable and unique illustration was produced around the time of the Lancaster Parliamentary election of 1895. It depicts the differing fortunes of two of the candidates: the losing Liberal, Isaac Saunders Leadam (1848–1913), and in the railway carriage, and heading for Westminster, the successfully elected Conservative, William Foster (1848–1908).

Leadam made five unsuccessful efforts to enter Parliament, of which Lancaster was the last; hence the title of the illustration, 'Missed It Again!' The artist is unknown, but it may have been produced by the Lancaster printer and publisher, Eaton & Bulfield.

In May 1900, Leadam was appointed Recorder of Grimsby and wrote several academic texts on law and history before his death. His opponent, William Foster, entered the family's textile business at Black Dyke Mills, Queensbury near Bradford, becoming a director in 1842. Before entering Parliament he was appointed Lord High Sheriff of Lancashire in 1891, and in 1892 became Deputy Lieutenant of the West Riding of Yorkshire.

The 1895 election was marred by allegations of corruption. A petition was lodged, suggesting that Foster and his election agents were guilty of bribery, including offering voters employment at Black Dyke Mills.[20] In the hearings at Lancaster Castle, Foster denied the charges, which were ultimately dismissed.[18] In the following election of 1900, he was defeated by a narrow margin, failing again in 1906 to secure the seat.

Missed It Again!
Illustration

Illustration from the 1895
Lancaster Parliamentary election

Printer: NA

1895

This souvenir brochure highlights the many historical and natural attractions of Lancaster, Morecambe and the surrounding area. The commentary is accompanied by illustrations, photographs, reproductions of drawings and paintings of the area, and a series of fine illustrations, the most outstanding of which is the one shown here depicting a view over Lancaster towards the Castle and the Priory. Perhaps more than anything, the publication of this brochure indicates the emerging tourist industry, and the degree to which leisure was playing an increasingly important part in the lives of people and the commerce of the region.

Illustration from a souvenir brochure concerning the attractions of Lancaster, Morecambe and the surrounding area

Printer: T. Johnson, Blackburn

1897

Souvenir of a Visit to Lancaster, its Castle, Church and Williamson Park. With Views of Morecambe and District Souvenir Brochure

The typeface 'Japanese' from a book auction catalogue of 1903 (p.119)

extended in the development of the later Ornamented forms

Ornamented type began to see significant use in publications during the early part of the nineteenth century, at a time when advertisement printing provided a new market for these inventive letterforms. Over the next century and a half, a myriad of designs emerged, which often reflected the preoccupations of their time, such as Orientalism and Art Deco.

Through the use of Ornamented type, printers sought to engage and please the public with new forms of lettering. Curling arms and swirling serifs, letters infilled with designs, outlined letters, Tuscans, shaded, and those with scrollwork, all form part of the broad category of Ornamented type.

The creation of the Modern and the Fat Face is seen by some[12] as the precursor to the development of this novel form of typography, initiating a freedom within type development that many designers embraced and

Examples found in a book auction catalogue of 1903 (p.119) include the letterform known as 'Japanese', as well as the revival and adapting of earlier forms such as the Blackletter.

The earliest example of Ornamented lettering in our Lancaster ephemera is found on the 1802 pamphlet in support of Napoleon Bonaparte (p.35). Here is ornamentation in one of its simplest

Catalogue, 1903 (p.119)

forms—as a shaded letter. Ink is partly omitted from the inside, while additional width is given to some strokes and stems to create the effect of a shadow being cast. It is a typeface that is probably derived from William Caslon IV's (1780–1869) type foundry and is highly effective in adding emphasis to the page. Shading is seen again in the elegant italics found on the election handbill of 1818 (p.43); a design that appears to originate from Edmund Fry's (1754–1835) foundry in Bristol.[7]

As Britain developed an increasingly consumer-driven economy, and advertisements became an integral part of everyday life, the diversity of lettering increased. Victorian printers, whose habit of using a multitude of lettering on their advertisements, made good use of these typefaces. We can see this approach in the item commemorating the opening of the Oddfellows Hall (1844, p.72), the lecture programme at the Athenaeum (1861, p.88), the opening of the Royal Albert Asylum (1868, p.90), the Rimmon Clayton bicycles advertisement (1893, p.105) and Petty's auction catalogue (1903, p.119).

Election handbill, 1818 (p.43)

The plans for the proposed market development (1894, p.106) has some particularly nice examples of Ornamented typefaces in a letterform

Pamphlet, 1802 (p.35)

(by William Caslon IV) with swirls and scrolling serifs that are clearly influenced by Art Nouveau, and another that is an adapted Blackletter (possibly the typeface known as *Memorial*, from Vincent Figgins' foundry in London). The printers of Lancaster appear to have embraced the use of Ornamented typefaces from an early point in their development.

The Ornamented typeface remained a commonly used tool of the commercial printer until its decline in the early twentieth century, when there developed a growing fascination with more restrained American typefaces, a popular interest in the revivalist typography of William Morris,[12] and the rise of Modernist typographic principles.

Typeface by William Caslon IV, from Architect's plan, 1894 (p.107)

ROYAL ALBERT ASYLUM

FOR IDIOTS AND IMBECILES OF THE NORTHERN COUNTIES, AT LANCASTER,

Programme, 1868 (p.90)

Palatine Hall on Dalton Square was built in 1779 as the first publicly visible Roman Catholic church after the Papist Act of 1778.[24][36] The act relieved some of the restrictions placed on Roman Catholics, including the right to build churches, though they could still not incorporate towers or bells. The design of this church in part reflects these continued restrictions, but the domestic design of the façade, with its fine Georgian proportions, also suggests a desire to construct a building that was as inconspicuous as possible. In 1859 the construction of the new Catholic cathedral, St. Peters, saw the Dalton Square building cease functioning as a church, and it was converted into a music hall and later a cinema.

At the time of this poster in 1900, the building was used as a public hall and venue for lectures (many of these being organised by the Storey Institute). The particular event advertised here, concerns the Transvaal, or Second Boer War (1899–1902), with the speaker presenting his talk with the assistance of a magic lantern illuminated by limelight. William Herbert-Jones, a popular circuit lecturer, journalist and Fellow of the Royal Geographical Society, travelled widely in Britain, Australia and New Zealand, lecturing on the history and geography of the British Empire, and was considered an exceptional public speaker.

After extensive remodelling in 1983, which included a new columned portico being added to the main entrance, the building was converted to Council offices.

Poster for a lecturer and lantern show on the Transvaal War at Palatine Hall

Printer: Unknown

1900

Mr Herbert-Jones on the Transvaal War Poster

PALATINE HALL, LANCASTER,

FRIDAY, MARCH 30th, 1900,

AT 7.45 P.M.

UNDER THE AUSPICES OF THE STOREY INSTITUTE LECTURE SOCIETY.

HIS WORSHIP, THE MAYOR,

WILL PRESIDE.

FRONT SEATS, **1s.** Back Seats and Centre Gallery, **6d.** Side Galleries, **3d.**

TICKETS AT STOREY INSTITUTE. AND "OBSERVER" OFFICE.

MR. HERBERT-JONES,

"One of the finest platform speakers in England."—STANDARD. F.R.G.S.,

ON THE

TRANSVAAL

 # WAR

WITH ABOUT 200 THRILLING LIMELIGHT PICTURES.

COPYRIGHT.

SEE HANDBILLS AND NEWSPAPERS.

William Atkinson & Sons were one of the earliest car dealers in the region; a trade facilitated by their large workshops and showrooms on North Road (now the Green Ayre pub) that were designed by the eminent local architects, Austin & Paley.[5] The diversification of the company in the early twentieth century from their original trade in bicycles to motorcars, illustrates the growing demand for this new form of transport.

The company made use of Lancaster's heritage by naming its motor car the *John O'Gaunt*, the title of the first Duke of Lancaster, third son of Edward III, and a prominent figure in the fourteenth century. Their marketing statement, which described their motor cars as being 'the greatest achievement we have ever had, gives the most satisfaction; a lady can manage them easily', is perhaps more indicative of the attitudes towards women at this time than anything else. Their trade mark, shown here, is taken from an advertisement found in a programme for a local bazaar of 1902.

William Atkinson & Sons, Manufacturers
Advertisement

Catalogue of a Small Library
Sales Catalogue

The Assembly Rooms, Kings Street, was the venue for this book auction of 1903, and relates to the sale of the collection of the late Mr Singer. The booklet is of somewhat poor quality but has some interesting typography on the cover, including elements that have a strong Art Nouveau influence as well as the use of Ornamented type. The company of G. H. (George Hardcastle) Petty, based in Market Street, were prominent auctioneers in Lancaster during the nineteenth and twentieth centuries.

The Assembly Rooms was originally built in 1759 to provide funds for the upkeep of the adjoining Penny's Almshouses. In addition to auctions it was used for a variety of events that included banquets, balls, fetes, and public meetings. It remains a place to buy books along with vintage clothes, bric-a-brac and collectables.

CATALOGUE

SMALL LIBRARY

About 1,500 Volumes,

COMPRISING

INCLUDING

Scarce and Valuable Topographical, Archæological, and
Antiquarian Books, and other Rare Books in
Miscellaneous Literature, many of which are
annotated by the late Mr. Slinger ;

ALSO

A number of Rare Old Prints, Pictures, and Maps
of Local Interest,

WHICH WILL BE REMOVED TO THE

ASSEMBLY ROOMS, KING STREET,

LANCASTER,

AND THERE SOLD BY AUCTION,

BY

G. H. PETTY,

ON TUESDAY, MARCH

The grocer T. D. Smith was established in Lancaster in 1858. They were to become one of Lancaster's most successful businesses, opening a string of premises and providing services such as home deliveries across the county.[33] A highly competitive firm, T. D. Smith developed a fierce rivalry with the local Co-operative Society, whose dividend system and ethos of 'strive to increase the good of all; thus only can the share of all increase' was anathema to the hard-nosed business sense of this local company. It was a battle between different philosophies; one based on entrepreneurial capitalism, the other on the idea of the co-operative commonwealth. T. D. Smith ceased trading in 1961, beaten by competition from rival grocers and the emergence of the culture of the supermarket.

This receipt, which also advertises the company's services, is a wonderful example of early twentieth century commercial design, with its elegantly constructed layout and typography, along with a number of illustrative elements.

Bill of sale for the grocer,
T. D. Smith

Printer: Unknown
1906

T. D. Smith, Grocer
Bill of Sale

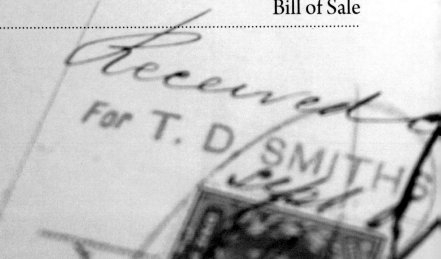

LANCASTER

190_

CENTRAL STORES
17 & 19, PENNY STREET

BRANCH STORES
IN EACH SUBURB.

O. SMITHS
LIMITED

BLENDERS,
PROVISION MERCHANTS
CONTRACTORS.

LIMITED.

HIPPODROME

Dalton Square, Lancaster.

PROPRIETOR AND MANAGER - - - - JOHN PORTER.

| 1st House. 7-0- | Monday, April 17th, 1911 AND DURING THE WEEK. | 2nd House. 9-0- |

Matinee, Monday, at 2-30. 2d., 4d., 6d.

HUNT & THOMAS

(MINNIE)   in Comedy Duologue entitled "Father Time," by Wal. PINK   (RHYS)

UNCLE'S OVERCOAT - Hippograph.

3 DELARIES 3

In their Speciality Act—"The Demon Grotto"

ROSE GOWER

The Popular Chorus Singer

Bros. LEO

Comedians

TWO LUCKY JIMS - Hippograph

FRANCE & STEWART

In their American Racing Comedy—"The 100 to 1 Chance"

Carl LYNN

King of Animal Mimics   From the Hippodrome and Coliseum, London

ORCHESTRA STALLS (First Five Rows), 1/-. No Early Door.

STALLS.	CIRCLE.	PIT.	Children under 15. STALLS - 3d. CIRCLE - 2d. PIT - 1d.
Pit 6d. Stalls	4d.	2d.	
Early Door, 9d.	Early Door, 6d.	Early Door, 3d.	Except Saturdays & Holidays

The First Two Rows, Centre Circle, 6d.; Early Door, 9d.

EARLY DOORS.—1st House. 6-15 to 6-45: 2nd House. 8-30 to 8-50.

No Half-price on Saturday Evenings. Seats not Guaranteed. No Money Returned. Cycles Stored.
This Hall is Disinfected with Jeyes' Fluid.   "Mail" Printing Works, 9, New St., Lancaster.

By 1911 Palatine Hall on Dalton Square, which was originally built as the Catholic Dalton Square Mission and then converted into a music hall, had become the Hippodrome, a theatre under the ownership and management of John Porter and W. J. Ferguson.[47]

This poster of 1911, details the entertainment on offer for the week beginning April 17th. The programme included acts such as the comedy dialogue of Hunt & Thomas, the duo France & Stewart and their American Racing Comedy, The Brothers Leo, songs by Rose Gower, the animal mimicry of Carl Lynn (from the Hippodrome and Coliseum, London), and the unusually named 3 Delaries and their Demon Grotto act.

Poster advertising acts appearing at the Hippodrome

Printer: Mail Printing Works

1911

The Hippodrome Poster

Lancaster Historical Pageant

1913

Souvenir

Lancaster Historical Pageant
Souvenir Programme

In August 1913 Lancaster held an historical pageant to
commemorate significant events from the town's past.
A script for the performance was written by the novelist
Halliwell Sutcliffe (1870–1932), and the performances
involved local people acting out a series of scenes from
Lancaster's history: from the arrival of the Romans to
the Jacobite Rebellion of 1745. The pageant, in which
over a thousand local people participated, was held in
Springfield Park, located off Ashton Road, in what is
now the grounds of Ripley St. Thomas School.[31]

The hand-drawn and illustrated cover design of the
programme carries the coat of arms of Lancaster and its
motto, Luck to Loyne: Loyne being an alternative name
for the River Lune that runs through the city. Inside,
a series of coloured drawings were used to illustrate
the scenes depicted in Sutcliffe's text. Unusually, the
programme was printed in York rather than Lancaster.

Cover of a souvenir programme
of events for the Lancaster
Historical Pageant

Printer: Ben Johnson & Co., York
1913

125

Waring & Gillow Cocktail Cabinet
Designer's Illustration

This designer's illustration for a cocktail cabinet was produced in 1930 by the renowned Lancaster furniture manufacturer, Waring & Gillow (formally Gillow & Co.). Established around 1770 by Robert Gillow (1704–1772), the company produced furniture of the highest standard, expanding from its original premises on Castle Hill to purpose-built showrooms and workshops on North Road in 1881.

The style of the cabinet has strong oriental influences: reflecting the continuing impact of this design approach on European art, architecture and furniture production during this period. While it is uncoloured, it includes details of the different woods to be used in the construction, giving us some idea of what the product might have looked like. Alongside mahogany, the cabinet was designed with bubinga, a wood found in equatorial Africa and used for veneers that has a colour ranging from pinkish red to a darker reddish brown. Macassar (ebony) was also to be included in the design. This dense wood originates from Indonesia and has a light, reddish brown body with darker brown or black stripes.

Waring & Gillow ceased trading in Lancaster in 1960. The North Road premises were used for a period in the mid-1960s as the temporary site of the city's newly established university. The building currently houses a number of businesses, including a nightclub.

Illustration for a cocktail cabinet by Waring & Gillow Ltd

Printer: NA

1930

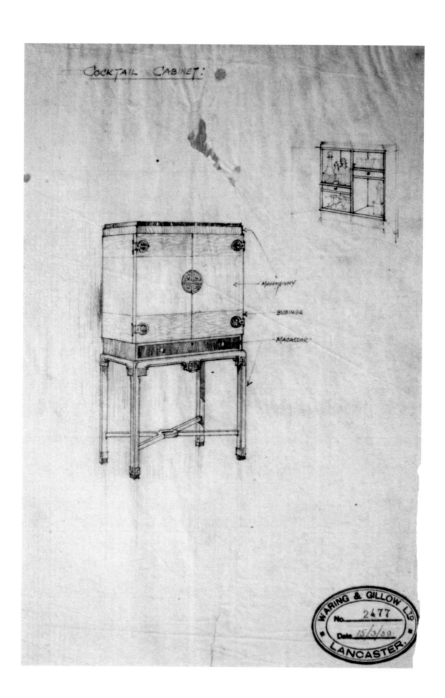

Cocktail Cabinet:

MAHOGANY

BUBINGA

MACASSAR

This document, detailing the plans for the creation of the new Public Library in Lancaster, was produced in 1931 by Borough Surveyor Frederick Hill. The Library was built in 1932 in a Neo-Georgian style of sandstone ashlar. The main entrance on Market Square that is shown in the drawing has a flat arch with the words PUBLIC LIBRARY in raised lettering. This is flanked by fasces and is placed beneath an open segmental pediment carried on Tuscan columns.[37]

Before its development as the Library, the site had housed a coaching inn (The Commercial Inn) as well as a police and fire station. More recently, the building was the focus of Lancashire Libraries' *Get It Loud in Libraries* project. Artists appearing here as part of that initiative included: the Grammy and Brit Award winner Adele, the Brit Award winner Florence and the Machine, and the Mercury nominated Bats for Lashes.

As well as the technical specifications of the development, the warm yellows and tans of the drawings reflect something of the colours of the stonework that was used to construct the building.

Lancaster Public Library
Architectural Plans

PUBLIC
LIBRARY

M

E

O

N

L

K
1·9 x 1·10 x 1·2

3·4 x 1·3 x 1·0

H

1·1 x 1·9
x 1·10

J

J

2·6 x 1·0 x 2·10

1·8 x 1·0 x 2·10

G

: Elevation of Main Entrance:

Plan:

Jectio
Main

The Rose Brand design was one of many produced by Storey Brothers at their oil cloth and table blaize works at White Cross Mills. Founded in 1848, Storeys became a major employer in Lancaster with an international reputation and market, while its senior figures became prominent local politicians and philanthropists. In 1895, Storey Brothers also established the commercial printing company Rembrandt Intaglio Printing under the direction of their former engraver Samuel Fawcett, who, along with Karel Klíč (1841–1926), were at the forefront of the development of gravure printing. Storey became the first firm to make rotogravure prints produced on rolls of paper at high speed,[9] and the products that utilised these designs were a common feature of households across the country and abroad.

Storey Brothers LTD: Rose Brand, Lancaster Cloth
Advertisement

TRADE MARK

REGISTERED

'ROSE BRAND

LANC

CL

TOREY BROS. & Co.

LIMITED
LANCASTER

STER
TH

Hedgehog RECORDS

We Buy and Sell Second-hand Records every Saturday on Lancaster Market Balcony

— COME AND SEE US! —

Hedgehog Records
Poster

Hedgehog Records was established in Lancaster in 1978 by husband and wife, Nick and Carol Hall, and Nick's sister, Jeni Hall. Renting a stall in Lancaster Market, Hedgehog specialised in new and used records, and soon tapped into a strong demand amongst local enthusiasts and students. Hedgehog's wide selection of vinyl, and the Halls' extensive knowledge of recorded music, created many loyal customers.

Local designer Chris Laver created the company logo: a sunglasses-wearing hedgehog together with bespoke typography. These details were included on the posters and packaging used to advertise the business. People liked the design so much that they often asked for the paper packaging bags, just so they could have a copy. Chris later moved to London where he developed a successful design business.

In October 1984 a fire devastated the Market, destroying the stall's entire stock and that of the other traders. After two months without a home, Hedgehog returned to the Market. The 'temporary' structure that was erected on the site would actually remain in place until 1995, when the Market was extensively remodelled. However, in 1997, less than two years after the redevelopment, Hedgehog decided to cease trading. The decline in demand for vinyl, along with the problems associated with the Market redevelopment, saw the end of this independent trader.

Screenprinted poster created for Hedgehog Records by the designer, Chris Laver

Printer: Chris Laver

1978

Formed in 1971 and housed in the former St Anne's Church on Moor Lane, The Dukes is a professional producing theatre that includes a cinema, art gallery and café bar. Its three auditoria include 'The Rake' (a studio theatre), 'The Round' (a 240 seat theatre space) and 'DT3' (a youth specific space). The Rake is also used for screening films, with a reputation for hosting independent cinema, and more recently, live broadcasts from venues such as Glyndebourne as part of the National Theatre Live initiative. Since 1986 the Dukes has also produced its highly regarded open-air theatre productions at the city's Williamson Park.

Screenprinted poster created for the Dukes by the Lancaster-based designer, John Angus

Printer: John Angus
1983

John Angus is amongst the artists commissioned by the Dukes to promote events (an example of his work is shown here). John is a Lancaster-based artist, designer, print-maker, researcher and curator. A major aspect of his work has been the production of posters for arts events, many of which he screen-prints by hand. He has undertaken hundreds of poster commissions for arts organisations throughout the UK: including the Arts Council England; Lancaster Litfest; the Royal Exchange Theatre, Manchester; the Royal Liverpool Philharmonic Orchestra; the Sherman Theatre, Cardiff; and the Young Vic, London. His posters are in several public collections, including the Victoria & Albert Museum. He was a leading member of the group of artists that formed the Storey Gallery in Lancaster in 1991, later becoming Co-ordinator, and then Director. He is currently running the company, now known as StoreyG2, delivering public realm projects.

The Dark Side of the Screen
Poster

Lancaster Musicians' Co-operative
Flyer

Unable to find anywhere to practise in Lancaster in the mid-1980s, a group of like-minded musicians decided to make their own arrangements and to provide other budding musicians from the Lancaster area with somewhere to play and be loud. This music collective opened up their own music studios in 1985 and through funding provided by the North West Arts Council, built two rehearsal rooms. The result was the Lancaster Musicians' Co-operative, which was opened at 1 Lodge Street as a non-profit making organization dedicated to providing musical services at affordable rates.

Flyer designed for the opening of the Lancaster Musicians' Co-operative

Printer: In-house

1985

The Lodge Street location is named after the family who sold the land to the architect Edmund Sharpe (1809–1877), the proprietor of the nearby Lancaster Athenaeum (now the Grand Theatre). The building housing the Co-operative was erected in 1883 by William Richmond as a coach works on land adjoining the theatre.[19]

Some of the previous users of the Co-op's facilities have included Paul 'The Rev' Mayers (Towers of London, The Prodigy), Mark Hunter (James), Tom English (Maximo Park), Keith Baxter (3 Colours Red), and the producer, Paul Tipler (Idlewild, Stereolab).

Twenty-nine years on, and the Lancaster Musicians' Co-operative is still giving bands somewhere to rehearse and record music, as well as providing the opportunity for its users to perform at specially organized events. It has also produced a series of CDs featuring the best of the area's music.

The flyer shown, complete with the Co-operative's original logo, was created for the opening of the studios in December 1985.

Carnival of Culture
Banner

Painted banner from the Carnival
of Culture celebration of
Lancaster's history and culture

Printer: NA

2008

In 2008, Lancaster City Council proposed to undertake a major redevelopment of a large area of the city that included the demolition of a number of historic buildings and the creation of a major new retail centre. The development plan met strong opposition from people across Lancaster who saw it as an act of economic and cultural vandalism. Many people not only doubted the economic benefits, but feared that the development would result in the loss of independent shops, more traffic problems and increased air pollution. The campaigners instead argued for an alternative approach that included a development proposal more in keeping with the city's size and needs.

As part of that campaign, the protestors organised the Carnival of Culture that sought to highlight Lancaster's strong historical and cultural heritage. A march though the city, followed by music and other events, helped to raise awareness about the issues around the development. At the public enquiry that was called in response to these concerns, the Council-supported development was rejected.

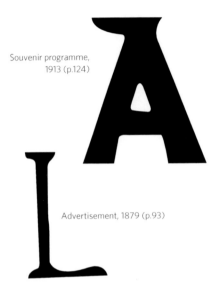

Souvenir programme, 1913 (p.124)

Advertisement, 1879 (p.93)

Flyer, 1985 (p.138)

While hand-drawn lettering can sometimes lack the geometric elegance of typefaces designed for books and other commercial printing, it can impart an originality that lends itself to the subject or the medium. The lettering examples seen in the Pageant brochure (1913, p.124), and the advertisements for Shrigley and Hunt (1879, p.93) and for Storey Brothers (1935, p.132), all work in this way. In the case of the last two examples, the hand-drawn lettering acts to emphasise the craft aspect of the company's work. In the case of Shrigley and Hunt, their advertisement seems to hark back to the medieval origins of ornamental glasswork. In the example

Poster, 1983 (p.137)

Banner, 2008 (p.141)

Map, 1891 (p.102)

River Lune

plate, and this plate then inked and pressed against paper to produce an image.

For many writers and designers hand-written scripts and notes remain a necessary part of the creative process even if the end product is digitally constructed. There remains for many, something important in the physicality of the page and the pen, regardless of the opportunities that digital technology brings.

of Storey Brothers, the lettering sits well with the hand-drawn nature of their textile designs. For some designers, a hand-crafted approach may be central to their practice (John Angus, p. 136), or forms a strong component of their work (Chris Laver, p.134).

Hand-drawn lettering might also be used out of necessity or convenience, such as when the medium requires a non-digital approach (Carnival of Culture banner: 2008, p.140), when resources are limited, or the design is composed of other hand-drawn elements like maps or plans (Library plans: 1931, p.129) and typeset or digitally constructed elements are neither feasible or necessary. In the case of the District Map of 1891 (p.100), the lettering, along with the map, would have been hand-engraved on to a metal

Poster, 1978 (p.134)

Advertisement, 1935 (p.132)

Reading
Poem draft

Draft of the poem *Reading* by
Lancaster poet Carole Coates.
First published in *Assent* 65/2

Printer: NA
2011

While digital media is an integral part of the construction and distribution of the work of artists, designers and writers, drafting and sketching by hand remains for many an important part of the creative process. Pen and paper continue to provide a remarkably simple and convenient way of working: one free from file formats, power supplies and system crashes.

Despite all of its advantages, what we lose in the use of the digital process, with its continuous overwriting of drafts, is an opportunity to see and revisit the process of revision, rethinking and the discarding of ideas that the hand-written approach provides. Here a draft of the poem *Reading* by Lancaster poet, Carole Coates, shows us this process: the lost words and lines, the reworked stanzas, the reconstructed passages. It is the creative process, captured in ink, graphite and wood pulp.

The poem was the winning entry for the 2011 Nottingham Open Poetry Competition, and is part of a longer verse novel sequence that is to be published by Shoestring Press in 2016.

~~he has~~

he ~~couldn't~~ it and he ~~couldn't~~ read

he couldn't read it and he could read it
he ~~could~~ can read lots of it anyway but it was hard
so grandpa reads ~~it to him~~ ~~the Huckleberry Finn~~
                    and they both ~~think~~ liked the river

he couldn't read it and he could read it
he can read lots of it anyhow but it's very hard
so grandpa reads it to him and they ~~both~~ ~~liked~~ about the river
_____

(he ~~couldn't~~ read it and he ~~could~~ read it
  he can read lots of it anyhow but it's ~~very~~ hard
  so grandpa reads it to him any evening

  ~~and~~ they ~~talk~~ about the Mississippi River
  ~~which is~~ big + brown and ~~rolling~~ like the Hudson
  although grandpa says ~~it~~ ~~has~~ to happen
                         he thinks it's

(~~but he does this each~~ ~~time~~
  sometimes he tries to read the book by himself
  ~~because~~ he likes Huck Finn ~~to too~~ who has a father
  she isn't there either but there's a footprint

  once someone has stood for a long time
  but this is as far as grandpa has read
  so he's cheating and looking ahead in the book

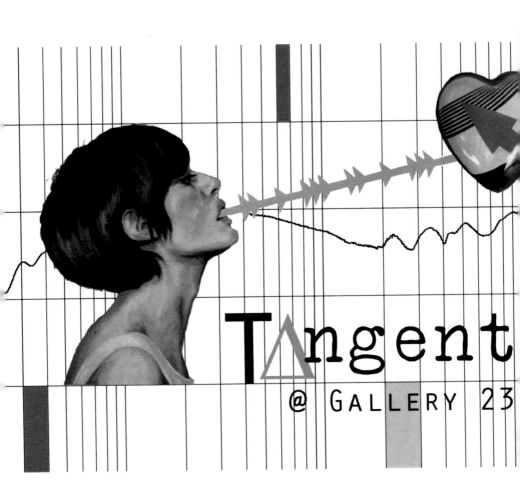

Arteria with Gallery 23 is an independent retailer of design-led gifts and a contemporary art gallery. The store is located on Lancaster's Brock Street in a restored nineteenth century building that won a Lancaster Design Award in 2007 for 'raising the game' in the city centre. The owner and founder of the business, Jane Richardson, is a Fine Art and Business Studies graduate, who in 2008 won Bay Business Centre and Lancaster Business Link's 'Business Woman of the Year Award'.

Gallery 23 on the first floor exhibits diverse arts and crafts showcasing established and up-and-coming artists and makers; most of whom are from the local area. The Arteria shop on the ground floor has products from national and international brands, and in Spring 2015, will celebrate 10 years of trading.

The company's continuously changing calendar of exhibitions and its evolving range of merchandise requires the frequent marketing of events and promotions. The printed and written marketing materials are designed by Sharon Burns, the General Manager of the business. Sharon studied textile design and has worked previously as a product designer and a design and trend consultant.

In 2012, Gallery 23 hosted an exhibition entitled Tangent, presenting the work of several local artists. The publicity material for the event was created by Sharon Burns, with an example of the work of artist and designer Lucy Pass featured on the front of the invitation and on an accompanying poster.

Invitation for artists' exhibition with example of the work of local artist and designer Lucy Pass

Printer: Printing.com, Lancaster; in-house

2012

Arteria with Gallery 23
Invitation/Poster

J. Atkinson & Co.
Packaging

Opposite: Modern packaging
for the company's products
that incorporates the original
grasshopper motif

Printer: In-house
2014

Below: The earliest known
example of a promotional item
produced by the company. It was
printed sometime between 1850
when Jane Atkinson took over
the running of the business, and
1854, when the company moved
from Cheapside to Castle Hill

Printer: Unknown

J. Atkinson & Co. have been supplying tea and coffee to the citizens of Lancaster since 1837, when Quakers Thomas Atkinson and his wife Jane founded *The Grasshopper Tea Warehouse* at Nos.1 & 2 Cheapside, offering teas 'equal to those sent from London'. The name for the business was based on the ancient Chinese proverb 'the grasshopper only eats the finest leaves'. Thomas died in the early 1850s and ownership passed to Jane who renamed it J. Atkinson & Co.

In 1854 the company moved to larger premises on the prestigious Castle Hill where the wholesale side of the company continued to grow. Following the deaths of Thomas and Jane, their son, Thomas (1844–), took over the running of the company. In addition to the coffee business, Thomas became a Borough magistrate, Freemason and Port Commissioner. In 1901 the expansion of the Storey Institute on Castle Hill caused the shop to move to its present location on China Street.

Thomas junior died in 1934 and ownership passed to their daughter Florence. The day-to-day running of the business was undertaken by Richard Marsden Riley. Richard was the son of Constance, Florence's sister and Richard Lister Riley. In 1960 Richard Marsden Riley and his wife Ann bought the business from Florence Atkinson. By 1989 the business had been inherited by Richard and Ann's daughter, Constance Anne, and she remained the proprietor until 2005 when the current owners, Ian and Sue Steel, bought the company.

J. Atkinson & Co. remain a tangible link to the city's mercantile past, with generations of continuous trading

Wholesale and Family Tea and Coffee Dealers.

WAREHOUSE.
J. ATKINSON & Co.,
Nos. 1 & 2, CHEAPSIDE,
Lancaster,
Where the Choicest Teas, Coffees, Fruits, &c., may be had at the
Lowest Market Prices.

J. Atkinson & Co.
COFFEE ROASTERS

J. ATKINSON & CO.
18 · 37
COFFEE ROASTERS

LANCASTER
BLEND TEA

BLACK TEA BLEND
African
Indian
Ceylon

Our time-honoured blend of African, Indian & Ceylon achieves a perfect balance of depth & clarity. Let it lift the gloom of a Winter's afternoon or slake the thirst on a Summer's day, it is both soothing & satisfying...

J. ATKINSON & CO.
18 · 37
COFFEE ROASTERS

ARCHETYPE
ESPRESSO BLEND

SUMATRAN
EL SALVADOR
GUATEMALAN
ETHIOPIAN

The bridge of the blend is built on flavours of roasted nut, dark chocolate, caramel and a melon softness offered up by our Centrals from Guatemala or El Salvador, while the Ethiopians from Primary Co-ops give us a light flurry of floral stone-fruit sweetness.

having resulted in an accumulation of wonderful artefacts in the China Street shop. These include tea canisters from the 1820s, an original spice drawer-run complete with uranium glass knobs, a 1930s tea blender, and from the same decade, two constantly working Whitmee Coffee Roasters. In the shop window the famous small roaster, an Uno dating from just after World War II, still wafts its delicious aroma out into the streets of Lancaster.

Over the last nine years the Steel family have sought to develop the business while maintaining the best of what they inherited. Innovative technology, new products, collaboration with other local businesses and an interest in the impact of the production process on their suppliers ('from bean to cup'), are all part of their approach.

In addition to the China Street shop the company has two cafés operating in the city: the Music Room in Sun Square that occupies the listed building of the same name (built c.1730), and The Hall, the converted Priory Hall designed by architects Paley and Austin in 1936 that adjoins the shop.

Ian and Sue's two sons, Caspar and Maitland, now work in the business, adding new energy, talent and ideas to the venture. Maitland has a degree in Fine Art and is the company's in-house designer, creating a range of marketing and packaging designs that include the original grasshopper motif, alongside contemporary typography. Caspar is the frontman, entering and winning barista competitions, and is responsible for training new members of the team to meet the company's high standards. The future of J. Atkinson & Co. is in the safe hands of a seventh generation.

APPENDIX:
THE RADICALS WONDERFUL SIX!!!

A NEW SONG
THE RADICALS WONDERFUL SIX!!!

Stay awhile my good friends while I sing you a song,
If it aint very witty - it aint very long,
'Tis only to "show up" as Wombwell would say,
The Radical SIX in a good humoured way.

First there's F—r, a *hair* in the "tail of the Lords"
Who the town's to astound with his *acts*, not his *words*;
By my faith, he's the man who will fathom what's rotten
For a hay stack he knows from a bag of Bow's Cotton.

Then there's R—l his colleague that "love" of a man.
Outrival his figure and grace if you can!
To quote his own words "he hard work will ne'er tire on"
For his body and soul are as tough as his iron.

Next a sweet cherub comes in the shape of G—e J—n,
Whose virtues, the saints say, bad men turn their backs on!
He vows the reform act with him shall ne'er halt,
Then be *his* first act to reform his own "Malt".

And there's G—l C—n the holy and godly,
Tho' the wags say that he, too, can act rather oddly;
Jocosely they hint that his *shoes* and the *weather*
Sympathise with each other, being both *bad* together.

With these there's the dealer in sweet things, J—n H—d
Whose talents henceforth will no more be concealed;
He'll be found on each question, a mighty *defence*,
For his no *meaning* words bother far more than *sense*.

Though B—ne's last, he should first have been named,
For amongst the whole SIX he is far the most famed;
He equally cares for God, devil and hope,
The idols he worships being candles and soap.

Then my boys, to the brim fill each sparkling glass,
And let this toast round the most merrily pass;
Since we hence shall be rid of Conservative tricks,
Drink success to the Radicals WONDERFUL SIX!!!

IMAGE CREDITS

Unless otherwise stated below, images are provided with the permission of Lancaster Public Library, located at Market Square, Lancaster, LA1 1HY.

John Angus   Image: p.137
w: http://www.johnangusposters.com
e: info@johnangusposters.com

Arteria with Gallery 23   Image: p.146
23, Brock Street, Lancaster, Lancashire LA1 1UR
w: www.arteriashop.co.uk

Carole Coates   Image: p.145
w: http://www.carolecoates.org.uk

Nick Hall   Image: p.134

Lancashire County Council   Image: p.83
Community Heritage, Lancashire Records Office,
Bow Lane, Preston, PR1 2RE
e: CH.enquiries@lancashire.gov.uk

Lancaster Musicians' Co-operative   Image: p.138
1, Lodge St, Lancaster LA1 1QW
w: http://www.lancastermusiccoop.co.uk
e: lancastermusiccoop@hotmail.co.uk

Chris Laver   Image: p.134

GLOSSARY

Art Deco: artistic and design style originating in Paris in the 1920s. It emphasised elegance, functionality, symmetry and modernity.

Arts & Crafts: international design movement existent mainly between 1860 and 1910. It was led by the artist William Morris (1834–1896) and architect Charles Voysey (1857–1941), and was influenced by the writings of Ruskin (1819–1900) and Pugin (1812–1852). It emphasised traditional craft skills, often employing decorative medieval, romantic or folk styles.

Art Nouveau: a style of art and architecture most prominent between 1890 and 1910, and inspired by natural forms and structures.

Assizes: criminal courts held periodically around England and Wales up until 1972.

Ashlar: dressed stonework with square edges and smooth faces.

Axis: an imaginary line drawn from top to bottom of a letter and bisecting the upper and lower strokes. For typefaces that show changes in the thickness of curved strokes, the inclination of the axis of the lowercase letter O is used as a defining characteristic.

Bauhaus: hugely influential multidisciplinary design movement founded in Weimar, Germany, in 1919. A key objective of the Bauhaus was to unify art, craft and technology. It operated until 1933 when, after a number of moves, it was forced to disband by the Nazis.

Blackletter: a letterform whose characteristics are derived from twelfth century manuscripts and which exhibit dramatic thin and thick strokes, and in some cases, elaborate swirling serifs. Also known as a Gothic.

Body Text: the main text content of a publication as opposed to titling, headlines and that found on the cover of the printed item.

Broadside Ballad: a single sheet of paper printed on one side, with a ballad or song and sometimes with a woodcut illustration.

Capital: the crowning part of a column or pilaster.

Cashiering: ritual dismissal from a position of responsibility as a result of a breach of conduct.

Chartism: political movement of the mid-1800s that agitated for political and voting reform.

Co-operative Commonwealth: a society based on co-operative and socialist principles.

Corinthian: a classical order of Greek and Roman architecture.

Counter: the enclosed or partially enclosed negative/white space of some letters.

Entablature: mouldings and bands that lie horizontally above columns, and resting on their capitals.

Didone: see Modern typeface.

De Stijl: design movement founded in the Netherlands in 1917 that emphasised simplicity of form and the use of primary colours.

Die Neue Typographie: typographic approach advocated by Jan Tschichold (1902–1974) and based on Modernist design rules.

Display Face/Text: type used at large sizes for headlines and titles.

Doric (typeface): see Sans Serif.

Ephemera: transitory items not meant to be retained or preserved.

Egyptian (typeface): see Slab Serif.

Fasces: a bundle of rods bound up with an axe in the middle. A symbol of the authority of ancient Rome.

Fat Face: a form of Modern typeface with extremely wide strokes and exaggerated contrast between thick and thin elements.

Freeman: a person who is entitled to certain political and social rights, including the right to vote.

Gothic (typeface): see Blackletter.

Gravure Printing: a type of printing process where an image is engraved onto a 'carrier' such as a cylinder. The depressions of the engraving are inked and the resulting image transferred to paper.

Grotesque (typeface): see San Serif.

Handbill: printed notice or advertisements to be distributed by hand or posted on a wall or window.

Higgler: an itinerant dealer of goods.

Huckster: a seller of small goods in a shop or stall; a pedlar or a hawker.

Humanist (typeface): having characteristics influenced by earlier, hand-drawn lettering that includes sloping cross-bars on the lowercase e, and low contrast between thick and thin strokes.

Italic: letters that slope to the right: often employed to emphasize or distinguish a word.

Jobbing Printing: printing of commercial and display work rather than books or newspapers.

Letterpress: printing process in which blocks of moveable type (metal or wood) are inked and pressed against paper in order to leave an impression.

Magic Lantern: a type of image projector developed in the 17th century where a light source is used to illuminate images painted onto glass slides.

Modern (typeface): typefaces with high and abrupt contrast between thick and thin strokes; unbracketed, hairline serifs and vertical axis. Also known as Didones.

Modernism: beginning in the late century, and perhaps more a way of thinking than a movement, it encompassed art, design and architecture amongst its many disciplines. Its characteristics may be said to include experimentation, industrialism, adoption of new technologies and simplicity of form.

Modillion (Cornice): an ornamented horizontal decorative moulding that crowns a building.

Monoline: lettering where strokes are uniform.

Old Face: typefaces whose origins date back to the mid-1400s and have features derived from calligraphy. Characterized by an inclined axis, limited contrast between thick and thin strokes and having serifs that are almost always bracketed.

Open Face: an ornamented typeface where the inside of the letter is 'open' so as to omit ink on printing, leaving only the outline of the letter and the counter visible.

Orientalism: imitation or depiction of aspects of Middle Eastern and East Asian cultures.

Ornamented (typeface): used for decorative purposes and titling, they often incorporate embellishments and illustrative elements.

Outlined (letterform): an ornamented typeface where additional lines are added outside the edge of the letter.

Palladian: a style of architecture derived from and inspired by the designs of the Venetian architect Andrea Palladio (1508–1580).

(Italian) Palazzo: a form of architecture based on the design of palazzi (palaces) built during the Italian Renaissance.

Pediment: the triangular section found above the horizontal structure (entablature), and usually supported by columns.

Pilaster: a projecting column built into or applied to the face of a wall. Most are commonly flattened or rectangular in form.

Point: a unit of type height. One point is approximately 0.35278mm, there being seventy-two points in one inch.

Portico: a formal entrance to a building, consisting of columns at regular intervals supporting a roof often in the form of a pediment.

Reform Acts: a series of Parliamentary acts introduced in the 1800s that enfranchised new groups of voters and sought to redistribute seats in the House of Commons.

Roman: a form of lettering with thick and thin strokes terminating in serifs.

Rotten Borough: a borough whose constituency had diminished significantly or ceased to exist, but which still retained the power to elect a Member of Parliament.

Sans Serif: a letter without serifs. Also known as a Grotesque or Doric.

Serif: semi-structural details on the ends of the strokes that make up letters, often in the form of decorative lines.

(Bracketed) Serif: a curved or wedge-like connection between the stem of a letter and the serif.

Sandstone: a sedimentary rock composed mainly of sand-sized minerals or rock grains.

Shaded (letterform): an ornamented typeface designed to imitate the effect of light falling on a letter as if to cast a shadow.

Shrievalty: the office, jurisdiction, or tenure of a sheriff.

Slab Serif: serifs that are thick or block-like. Also known as an Egyptian.

Stem: the main, usually vertical stroke of a letter.

Stroke: the main diagonal part of a letter, such as in N, M, or Y.

Stress: the transition between thick and thin strokes.

Terminal: the end of any stroke of a letter.

Transitional (typeface): typefaces that have characteristics that include marked contrast between thick and thin strokes, more upright stress in letters and serifs that tend towards horizontal.

Transvaal Wars: known also as the Boer Wars, they were fought from 1880 until 1881, and again from 1899 until 1902, in a conflict between British Imperial forces and Afrikaner settlers in what is now South Africa.

Tuscan: a classical order of architecture with limited ornamentations. In relation to lettering, it refers to embellishments including bulges on stems and strokes, or split terminals.

Typeface: a set of printing type of a particular design.

Type Founder: one who founds or casts metal type.

Type Foundry: a company that manufactures and distributes typefaces.

Venetian Gothic: an architectural style combining the use of the Gothic arch with Byzantine and Moorish architectural influences.

Victorian: architectural styles employed predominantly during the middle and late nineteenth century.

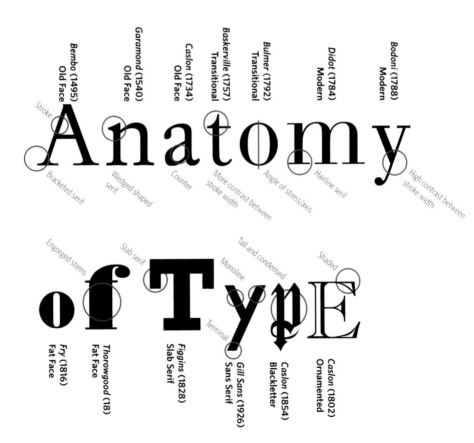

SOURCES OF INFORMATION

PUBLICATIONS

1. Alston, J. (1992) *The Royal Albert: Chronicles of an Era*. Lancaster: Centre for Northwest Regional Studies, Lancaster University.
2. Bartram, A. (2007) *Typeforms: A History*. London: British Library.
3. Benson, J. H. and Carey, A. J. (1940) *The Elements of Lettering*. New York: McGraw-Hill.
4. Betjemman, A. G. (2007) *The Grand Theatre Lancaster: Into the Third Century*. Lancaster: Lancaster Footlights Club.
5. Brandwood, G. *et al*. (2012) *The Architecture of Sharpe, Paley and Austin*. London: English Heritage.
6. Catt, J. (1988) *A History of Lancaster's Market*. Local Studies No.7: Lancaster: Lancaster City Museum.
7. Chambers, D. (Ed.) (1986) *Specimen of Modern Printing Types by Edmund Fry, 1828*. London: Printing Historical Society.
8. Chase, M. (2007) *Chartism: A New History*. Manchester: Manchester University Press.
9. Christie, G. (1964) *Storeys of Lancaster, 1848-1964*. London: Collins.
10. Dowding, G. (1998) *Introduction to the History of the Main Stages in the Development of Typeface Design from 1440 to the Present day*. London: British Library.
11. Fleury, C. (1891) *Time-honoured Lancaster: Historic Notes on the Ancient Borough of Lancaster*. Lancaster: Eaton & Bulfield Printers.
12. Gray, N. (1938) *Nineteenth Century Ornamented Types and Title Pages*. London: Faber & Faber.
13. Hansard, T. C. (1825) *Typographia: An Historical Sketch of the Origin and Progress of the Art of Printing*, London: Baldwin, Cradock, and Joy.
14. Hart, H. (1900) *Notes on a Century of Typography at the University Press, Oxford 1693-1794*. Oxford: Oxford University Press.
15. Howson, G. (2008) *The Making of Lancaster: People, Places and War, 1789-1815*. Lancaster: Palatine Books.
16. Irving, R. (1987) *Lancaster Past and Present*. Manchester: Neil Richardson.
17. Johnson, A. F. (1970) *Selected Essays on Books & Printing*. Amsterdam: Hes & De Graff.
18. *Judgment was delivered yesterday in the Lancaster election petition. The Times* (London). 25 January 1896, p.9.
19. Lancaster City Council & English Heritage (2012) *Lancaster Corridor North: Assessment of Heritage Values and Significance*: Cirencester: The Conservation Studio.
20. *Lancaster Election Petition. The Times* (London). 15 January 1896. p.7.
21. Lawson, A. S. (2010) *Anatomy of a Typeface*. Boston: David R. Godine.
22. Lund, R. (2012) *Ridicule, Religion and the Politics of Wit in Augustan England*. Farnham: Ashgate Publishing.
23. Mosley, J. (1999) *The Nymph and the Grot: The Revival of the Sanserif Letter*. London: Friends of St. Bride Printing Library.
24. North West Regional Development Agency (2010) *Discover Sacred Lancaster: A Walk of 2000 years*.
25. Pickering, A. (2008) *Feargus O'Connor*. London: The Merlin Press Ltd.
26. Price, J. (1998) *Sharpe, Paley and Austin: A Lancaster Architectural Practice 1836-1942*. Lancaster: Centre for Northwest Regional Studies, Lancaster University.
27. Read, D. (1973) *Peterloo: The 'Massacre' and Its Background*. Manchester: Manchester University Press.
28. Stone, I. (1979) Profile: William Parker Snow, 1817-1895. *Polar Record*, No.19, Vol.119, pp.116–119. Cambridge: University of Cambridge Press.

29. Updike, D. E. (1962) *Printing Types: Their History and Use*. Vol. II. Cambridge: Harvard University Press.

30. Waters, W. (2003) *Stained Glass from Shrigley and Hunt of Lancaster and London*. Lancaster: Centre for Northwest Regional Studies, Lancaster University.

31. White, A. (2003) *Lancaster: A History*. West Sussex: Phillimore Ltd.

32. White, A. (2009) *Lancaster's Historic Inns*. Lancaster: Carnegie Publishing.

33. Winstanley, M. (1991) *A Traditional Grocer: T. D. Smith's of Lancaster, 1858-1981*. Lancaster: Lancaster University, Centre for North West Regional Studies, (Occasional Papers).

WEBSITES AND ONLINE RESOURCES

34. British Banking History Society. *British Banking History Society* [online] Available at: *http://www.banking-history.co.uk/lancaster.html* [Accessed 12 Sep 2012].

35. British History Online. *A History of the County of Cambridge and the Isle of Ely: Volume 3: The City and University of Cambridge* [online] Available at: *http://www.british-history.ac.uk/report.aspx?compid=66637* [Accessed 24 May 2013].

36. British Listed Buildings. *Palatine Hall, Lancaster* [online] Available at: *http://www.britishlistedbuildings.co.uk/en-383129-palatine-hall-lancashire* [Accessed 22 Jun 2013].

37. British Listed Buildings. *Public Library, Lancaster* [online] Available at: *http://www.britishlistedbuildings.co.uk/en-383210-public-library-lancashire* [Accessed 01 May 2012].

38. Florence, A. M. *Some Liverpool Firsts in Medicine* [online] Available at: *http://www.evolve360.co.uk/Data/10/Florence.pdf* [Accessed 04 Aug 2014].

39. Gilchrist Education Trust. *History* [online] Available at: *http://www.gilchristgrants.org.uk/New_Folder/history.htm* [Accessed 02 Aug 2014].

40. Higginbottom, P. (2014) *The Workhouse, Lancaster* [online] Available at: *http://www.workhouses.org.uk/Lancaster* [Accessed 17 Dec 2012].

41. Institute of Historical Research. *Lancaster* [online] Available at: *http://www.historyofparliamentonline.org/volume/1820-1832/constituencies/lancaster* [Accessed 30 Mar 2013].

42. Institute of Historical Research. Liverpool [online] *http://www.historyofparliamentonline.org/volume/1690-1715/constituencies/liverpool* [Accessed 04 Uag 2014].

43. Lancaster City Council. *Lord Ashton: Lino King* [online] Available at: *http://www.lancaster.gov.uk/council-and-democracy/civic-ceremonial/lord-ashton-lino-king/* [Accessed 04 Sep 2012].

44. Olinger, J. P. *The Guano Age in Peru* [online] Available at: *http://www.historytoday.com/john-peter-olinger/guano-age-peru* [Accessed 07 May 2014].

45. National Library of Scotland. *Broadside Ballad entitled Ye Mariners of England* [online] Available at: *http://digital.nls.uk/broadsides/broadside.cfm/id/14758* [Accessed 07 June 2013].

46. Raven, J. London Booksites: *Places of Printing and Publishing before 1800*. [online] Available at: *http://www.bl.uk/whatson/panizzi3final.pdf* [Accessed 17 July 2014].

47. Theatres Trust. *Hippodrome, Lancaster* [online] Available at: *http://www.theatrestrust.org.uk/resources/theatres/show/175-hippodrome-lancaster* [Accessed 02 Oct 2013].

48. Thorne, N. (2013) *The Road Across Lancaster Sands*. [online] Available at: *http://www.bodian.co.uk/uploads/1/2/9/3/12937126/cross_sands_links_and_information_for_website.pdf* [Accessed 20 Dec 2013].

LIBRARIES, MUSEUMS AND ARCHIVES

Lancashire Records Office, Bow Lane, Preston, Lancashire, PR1 2RE.

Lancaster City Museum, Market Square, Lancaster, LA1 1HT.

Lancaster Community Heritage Centre, New Street, Lancaster, LA1 1EG.

Lancaster Public Library, Market Square, Lancaster, LA1 1HY.

ACKNOWLEDGEMENTS

I would like to express my thanks to Bev Kain and Mick Murphy for their encouragement, advice and support in the development of this publication. Also, I would like to thank the local businesses, organisations and individuals who helped in providing examples of ephemera and the accompanying information about their work. In particular: poet Carole Coates, Ian Steel of J. Atkinson & Co., David Blackwell and Ian Dicken from Lancaster Musicians' Co-operative, Sharon Burns and Jane Richardson from Arteria and Gallery 23, artist and designer Lucy Pass, and in relation to the item from Hedgehog Records, Nick and Jeni Hall, and designer Chris Laver. Finally, and not least, I am indebted to the staff at Lancaster Public Library and at Lancashire County Council's Cultural Services for their help in researching this work and for the permission given to include details from historic documents and photographs. The Cultural Services Team and Lancashire Libraries are invaluable sources of information, expertise and research, and I would like once again to extend my admiration and thanks for the work they do in preserving and enhancing the heritage of Lancaster and the County of Lancashire. The value of public libraries and archives is measured not only in the resources they hold, whether paper or electronic, or their contribution to the economy, which is significant, but in their ability to open up new worlds, ideas and ways of seeing to anyone who cares to look.

Simon Hawkesworth
Lancaster
2014